Elite • 113

US Navy SEALs

Mir Bahmanyar • Illustrated by Michael Welply

Consultant editor Martin Windrow

First published in 2005 by Osprey Publishing
Midland House, West Way, Botley, Oxford OX2 0PH, UK
443 Park Avenue South, New York, NY 10016, USA
Email: **info@ospreypublishing.com**

A CIP catalog record for this book is available from the British Library

ISBN 1 84176 807 3

CONSULTANT EDITOR: Martin Windrow
Editor: Neil Maxwell
Design: Alan Hamp
Index by Alan Thatcher
Originated by The Electronic Page Company, Cwmbran, UK
Printed in China through World Print Ltd.

05 06 07 08 09 10 9 8 7 6 5 4 3 2

FOR A CATALOG OF ALL BOOKS PUBLISHED BY
OSPREY MILITARY AND AVIATION PLEASE CONTACT:

Osprey Direct USA, c/o MBI Publishing
P.O. Box 1, 729 Prospect Ave, Osceola, WI 54020, USA
E-mail: **info@ospreydirectusa.com**

Osprey Direct UK
PO Box 140, Wellingborough, Northants, NN8 2FA, UK
E-mail: **info@ospreydirect.co.uk**

www.ospreypublishing.com

Acknowledgments

Special thanks to Sara van Valkenburg, Buck Springwater, Chris
Osman of Tactical Assault Gear, and Lieutenant Kathy Sandoz,
US Navy, Deputy Director of Public Affairs.

Artist's note

Readers may care to note that the original paintings from which
the color plates in this book were prepared are available for private
sale. All reproduction copyright whatsoever is retained by the
Publishers. All enquiries should be addressed to:

michael.welply@wanadoo.fr

The Publishers regret that they can enter into no correspondence
upon this matter

US NAVY SEALS

INTRODUCTION

No other American special operations force has drawn as much media attention as the modern-day United States Navy SEALs. The SEALs, which stand for Sea, Air and Land, were created by Presidential Order on January 8, 1962. President John F. Kennedy, a former Navy officer, envisioned a greater unconventional war-fighting capability for the military in its struggle against the real and perceived enemies of the United States. The SEALs' intended purpose was to conduct military operations in maritime and riverine environments, the staple since World War Two for naval frogmen and Underwater Demolition Teams (UDT). The original members of SEAL Teams One and Two were recruited out of the UDTs, a branch which continued to exist for another two decades. The naval commandos fought in the Vietnam War from 1966 to 1973. On May 1, 1983, all remaining UDTs were redesignated as SEAL Teams or Swimmer Delivery Vehicle Teams (SDVTs). Since then, the SDVTs have been redesignated as SEAL Delivery Vehicle Teams.

The United States was perceived as weak after the political and military debacle in Vietnam (1962–75) where seemingly one of the world's two superpowers was defeated by a simple people's movement. The catastrophic result of a failed hostage rescue in Iran in 1980 during Operation *Desert One*, compounded by the mixed outcome of special operations missions during the invasion of Grenada under Operation *Urgent Fury* in 1983, brought about a reevaluation of commando operations. In an effort to repair the conventional weaknesses so cruelly exposed in Southeast Asia, the US military created a separate branch for its elite units. Policy-makers also recognized the threat of a geo-political shift after the Soviet Union invaded the sovereign state of Afghanistan in 1979 with little international resistance. Since open warfare with the Communist bloc was unthinkable, a reevaluation of military strategy led to the creation of an all-encompassing command for US special operations forces.

Considered one of the all-time classic underwater frogmen/SEALs photos. Basic training includes ocean swims of up to two miles while wearing fins, and classes on basic small-boat skills. However, because of the growing demands on US military forces during the Global War on Terrorism, Naval Special Warfare forces are tasked with multi-component missions not necessarily associated with their original purpose of operating in riverine and maritime environments.

3

The United States Special Operations Command (USSOCOM) was activated on April 16, 1987, and since its inception has been located at MacDill Air Force Base, Florida. USSOCOM promoted the advancement of officers within the special operations field, and allowed well-trained enlisted members to spend the majority of their careers within the elite community. USSOCOM's assets include special operations units from all branches of the American military: the Army, Air Force, Navy and, most recently, elements of the Marine Corps.

NAVAL SPECIAL WARFARE COMMAND 1987–2004

The Naval Special Warfare Command (NAVSPECWARCOM), commissioned on April 16, 1987, at the Naval Amphibious Base at Coronado, San Diego, California, is the naval component to the United States Special Operations Command. Naval Special Warfare (NSW) personnel comprise less than one percent of the entire US Navy. NSW forces conduct five principal missions in special operations, although more specific tasks have been assigned in the wake of the Global War on Terrorism (GWOT).

The five principal mission categories are: unconventional warfare, direct action, special reconnaissance, foreign internal defense, and combating terrorism. Additional mission tasks include security assistance, anti-terrorism (now a priority), counter-drug, personnel recovery, and special activities.

Naval commandos have participated with mixed results in numerous military operations since 1983, including Operations *Urgent Fury* (Grenada 1983), *Earnest Will* (Persian Gulf 1987–90), *Just Cause* (Panama 1989–90), *Desert Shield/Desert Storm* (Middle East/Persian Gulf 1990–91), *Enduring Freedom* (Afghanistan, from 2001) and *Iraqi Freedom* (Iraq, from 2003). NSW missions in Somalia, Bosnia, Haiti, and most recently in Liberia, the Philippines, and the Horn of Africa, have received less attention.

The major operational components of NSW Command include Naval Special Warfare Groups One and Three at Coronado, commonly referred to as the West Coast Teams. Naval Special Warfare Groups Two and Four, stationed in Norfolk, Virginia, are known as the East Coast Teams. As common with special operations forces, these groups have an intense rivalry. NSW forces total 6,600 members, of whom 5,400 are active-duty, including 2,450 SEALs and 600 Special Warfare Combatant Craft Crewmen (SWCC), and more than 1,200 are reservists, including 325 SEALs, 125 SWCC and 775 support personnel. In contrast, the 75th Ranger Regiment, the "warriors" of the US Army, numbers approximately 2,000 pure "trigger-pullers" and no reserve component. NSW's ever-increasing size has resulted in some budgetary growing pains due to the competition for funding among the military branches. Nonetheless, a basic axiom holds true – the larger the force, the more difficult it is to

A SEAL feeds chum to Zak, a 375lb California sea lion, between his many training swims organized as part of the Shallow Water Intruder Detection System (SWIDS) program at the Space and Naval Warfare Systems Center on January 29, 2003. Zak has been trained to locate swimmers near piers, ships, and other objects in the water considered suspicious and a possible threat to military forces. The SWIDS program was used to support missions under Operation *Enduring Freedom*.

remain elite due to the challenges of finding and keeping recruits who can maintain high standards.

BASIC UNDERWATER DEMOLITION/SEAL (BUD/S)

All Navy personnel, officer and enlisted alike, who desire to become naval commandos must attend the Basic Underwater Demolition/SEAL (BUD/S) course conducted at the Naval Special Warfare Center, Coronado.

To qualify to attend the course, candidates must swim 500 yards using breast- and/or sidestroke in less than 12 minutes 30 seconds. They are allowed a 10-minute rest before having to perform a minimum of 42 push-ups in two minutes, before taking a two-minute break. Next comes at least 50 sit-ups in two minutes, again followed by a two-minute rest, and then a minimum of six pull-ups, with no time limit. After resting for ten minutes they have to tackle a 1½-mile run wearing boots and long pants, in under 11 minutes 30 seconds.

BUD/S begins with an indoctrination program in which the students must meet the minimum physical requirements and learn rudimentary skills needed for the actual course. BUD/S has three distinct phases:

First phase: Basic Conditioning

First Phase is eight weeks long and emphasizes increased physical conditioning for students, including weekly four-mile runs in boots as well as timed obstacle courses. The student will also take part in ocean swims of up to two miles while wearing fins. Rudimentary training also includes classes on basic small-boat skills. The initial four weeks of First Phase are preparation for the fifth week, commonly known as "Hell Week." Students undergo five and a half days of continuous training, with no more than four hours of sleep during the week. Hydrographic surveying and the preparation of hydrographic charts are taught over the remainder of the BUD/S First Phase.

Second phase: Diving

Scuba (self-contained underwater breathing apparatus) training consists of two types – open circuit (compressed air) and closed circuit (100 percent oxygen). This is considered by many to be the SEALs' *raison d'être*, and accordingly lasts eight weeks.

Third phase: Land Warfare

This part lasts nine weeks and teaches basic field craft, demolition, reconnaissance, weapons, and tactics. BUD/S concludes with a practical tactical exercise at San Clemente Island, off the San Diego coast.

Additional training lasting from six months to one year has been necessary before an officer is considered fully qualified. The practice has been for BUD/S graduates to go on to complete a three-week course in standard airborne training at the US Army Airborne School at Fort Benning, Georgia. Once these courses have been completed the new commandos are assigned to a SEAL Team

A Naval Special Warfare Combatant Craft Crewman fires his .50-cal. machine gun from a rigid hull inflatable boat while operating at a forward location in the Central Command Area of Responsibility on February 18, 2003. A RHIB is a high-speed, high-buoyancy, extreme weather craft whose main role is ship-to-shore insertion/extraction of SEAL tactical elements. Lightly loaded, it has been able to operate in winds of up to 45 knots. There are two types of RHIB in use, a 24ft version and a 30-footer.

Members of Basic Underwater Demolition (BUD/S) Class 244 endure the bitter cold while taking part in exercises as part of their BUD/S confidence and personal endurance training at the Naval Amphibious Base, Coronado, in 2003.

for a probationary period, where more training is undertaken in the form of a three-month SEAL tactical training (STT) course. After completing STT, SEALs are then assigned to either an operational SEAL platoon or SEAL Delivery Vehicle (SDV) Task Unit for their initial operational assignment. After successfully passing a probationary period, the SEAL announces that he is a fully fledged member of the SEAL platoon by pinning on his "Trident," the Naval Special Warfare Insignia.

In 2003/04 NAVSPECWARCOM released this BUD/S training timeline: indoctrination, five weeks; basic conditioning, eight weeks; diving, eight weeks; land warfare, nine weeks; basic parachute training, three weeks; special operations technician training, two weeks at the Naval Special Warfare Center, followed by 18-D, an intense course of instruction in medical skills (hospital corpsmen only); assignment to SEAL team for six to 12 months of on-the-job training; then receive NSW classification, a SEAL Naval Enlisted Classification (NEC) code.

ADVANCED SEAL TRAINING

BUD/S graduates receive three weeks basic parachute training at the Army Airborne School, Fort Benning, then return to the Naval Special Warfare Center, Coronado, for SEAL qualification training (SQT). Navy corpsmen (medics) who complete BUD/S and basic airborne training also attend two weeks of special operations technician training at Coronado before SQT. (Naval commandos may no longer need to attend the Army Airborne School as the Navy has developed a highly compressed version of the standard Army three-week airborne course and the advanced military free-fall program.)

Members of SEAL Delivery Vehicle Team One, accompanied by US Air Force Brigadier General Gregory L. Trebon (in black), Commander, Special Operations Command Pacific, conduct a free-fall parachute training jump from a US Army UH-60L Black Hawk helicopter from over 10,000ft above Ford Island, Hawaii, on March 12, 2003. General Trebon received much criticism for the handling of special operations missions in support of Operation *Anaconda*, Afghanistan, 2002.

SQT is a 15-week course designed to produce qualified SEAL operators by providing the full spectrum of basic and advanced individual skills and small unit training. Topics include: combat medical, communications, land navigation, marksmanship, close-quarters defense and combat, tactics, demolition, maritime operations, combat swimming, and tactical parachuting. At the conclusion of SQT (and more than a year of training), a successful student is awarded a SEAL Naval Enlisted Classification (NEC) code and Trident warfare pin. Then, before reporting to their first operational NSW command, new SEALs attend the three-week NSW basic cold weather maritime training course in Kodiak, Alaska.

SEALs assigned to SEAL Delivery Vehicle Teams will attend additional training in Panama City, Florida, before reporting to their teams. SDV units are tasked with all aspects of combat submersible systems, including the Dry Deck Shelter which allows for the launch and recovery of a SEAL Delivery Vehicle or Combat Rubber Raiding Craft (CRRC) with personnel from a submerged specially configured submarine. Other missions assigned to SDV units are port and harbor anti-shipping attacks/raids, hydrographic reconnaissance, and other intelligence-gathering missions. Special operations forces (SOF) can depend on SDV units for resupply as well.

Corpsmen will leave Coronado and take part in an intense course of instruction in medical skills called 18-D (Special Operations Medical Sergeant Course). Over 30 weeks students receive training in burns, gunshot wounds, and trauma. All other SEALs will report to an operational SEAL team in either Virginia or California and begin 18 months of training in preparation for an overseas deployment. Advanced courses include explosives, diving supervisor, language training, sniper, and communications. SEALs can and do still attend various additional Army courses, such as Ranger and Pathfinder schools.

Archetypal SEAL missions include the destruction or sabotage of enemy facilities on land and at sea. Traditional commando tasks also involve the disruption of lines of communication and intensive reconnaissance work. Akin to their US Army Special Forces counterparts, the Green Berets, Navy SEALs are also tasked with working closely with other military and paramilitary units in organization, training, and other military needs required by indigenous forces. Due to the very high-risk nature of special operations, SEALs depend on higher naval components for support. SEAL platoons are lightly armed and equipped, and therefore cannot sustain any lengthy period of combat.

Special Warfare Combatant Craft Crewmen (SWCC) operate and maintain an inventory of state-of-the-art high-performance boats and ships used to support special operations missions. Combat crewmen are assigned to Special Boat Units/Teams (SBUs). A combat crewman attends advanced training at the Naval Special Warfare Center. SBU members may be parachute-qualified and may receive additional training in weapons, tactics, and techniques. However, their primary focus is on the clandestine infiltration and exfiltration of commandos in maritime and riverine areas. They can also provide firepower from their vessels, conduct coastal patrols, and surveillance. Harassment and interdiction of maritime lines of communication is another primary task. Missions may also include foreign internal defense and deception operations, search and rescue, and armed escort.

There are minimum physical requirements for attending the SWCC training course. Participants must swim 500 yards using breast- and/or sidestroke in under 13 minutes. They then rest for ten minutes before performing a minimum of 42 push-ups in two minutes, with a two-minute rest. Then comes a minimum of 50 sit-ups, again in two minutes, with a two-minute rest. At least six pull-ups with no time limit are followed by a ten-minute rest, before a run of 1½ miles in running shoes in under 12 minutes 30 seconds.

This is how NAVSPECWARCOM describes the Special Warfare Combatant Craft Crewmen course.

1. Physical fitness
The training is designed to develop a high level of stamina and endurance to prepare the student for the demands of the maritime combat environment.

Naval Special Warfare Combatant Craft Crewmen from a rigid hull inflatable team operate with a Mark V Special Operations Craft (SOC) at a forward location in the Central Command Area of Responsibility on February 18, 2003. The SOC is the newest, versatile, high-performance combatant craft introduced into the NSW Special Boat Squadron inventory. Its typical mission lasts 12 hours.

San Diego-based Special Warfare Combatant Craft Crewmen and SEALs train members of the Philippine Armed Forces aboard a rigid hull inflatable at Zamboanga, April 20, 2002. NSW operators were conducting joint training with the AFP in support of Operation *Enduring Freedom.*

2. Swimmer skills
Will develop the student's confidence in his ability to survive in the ocean, and if necessary to assist a crewmate under adverse conditions.

3. First aid skills
Basic first aid and dealing with medical emergencies in a combat environment are covered.

4. Maritime navigation skills
The student undergoes extensive training in piloting, dead reckoning, electronic navigation and Rules of the Road, to prepare them in all aspects of voyage planning and execution of long-range maritime operations.

5. Basic seamanship skills
Classroom instruction and practical work in basic boat handling and knot tying prepares the student to operate a Special Warfare Combatant Craft under supervision, in restricted waters and open ocean. These high-performance craft are designed to operate at speeds of up to 40 knots in rough sea conditions.

6. Engineering skills
Classroom instruction and practical work prepares the student to operate and monitor the following engineering systems: propulsion (internal combustion engines, jet drives, and out drives), fuel sea water cooling, bilge pumping, steering, electrical, hydraulics, and damage control.

7. Communications skills
A radiotelephone operator is the critical link between the combat element and the outside world; how well he performs this function will in many cases determine the success of the mission. This unit prepares the student for planning and establishing viable communications during an NSW mission.

8. Warfare skills
Care and maintenance of combat gear and basic tactical employment of Special Warfare Combatant Craft is covered in this unit.

9. Weapons skills
Students learn proper handling, disassembly, cleaning, assembly, and operation of small arms ranging from .357 Magnum revolvers to .50-cal. machine guns.

ORGANIZATION OF US NAVAL SPECIAL OPERATIONS FORCES

The structure of US naval special operations forces is described in the US Army Command and General Staff College's *The Special Operations Forces Reference Manual* of 1999/2000.

Naval Special Warfare Center

The Naval Special Warfare Center, Naval Amphibious Base Coronado, is commanded by a Captain (O-6), and is the schoolhouse for NSW training. The 26-week BUD/S course is held here as well as the nine-week Special Warfare Combatant Crewman (SWCC) course. It is also the venue for advanced maritime special operations training. A detachment is maintained at NAB Little Creek, Virginia, for the training of East Coast personnel.

Naval Special Warfare Development Group

The Naval Special Warfare Development Group, based at Little Creek, is commanded by a Navy Captain (O-6). It tests, evaluates, and develops current and emerging technology, and also develops maritime, ground and airborne tactics.

Naval Special Warfare Groups

Two NSW Groups, One and Two, are based at NABs Coronado and Little Creek, under the command of Echelon 2 captains (O6). Their role is to equip, support, and provide command and control elements. They provide SEAL and SDV platoons and forces. They are organized into three SEAL teams, each composed of eight 16-man platoons; one SDV team; and small command and control elements outside the continental United States, to support NSW forces during operations.

Naval Special Warfare Command Combat Service Support Teams (CSST)

One CSST is assigned to each NSW Group, and has three main mission elements: (operational) PLAN/CON (tingency) PLAN and crisis-action logistic planning and coordination; in-theater contracting, small purchase and lease actions; and forward operating base support. Additional tasks include force embarkation; load-planning; multi-modal transport coordination; combat cargo handling; in-theater logistic coordination; and exercise

US Naval Special Warfare Command – Organizational Chart.

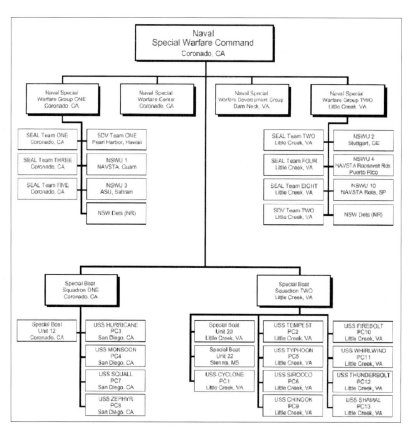

related construction. Its roles also cover infrastructure support; contingency engineering; expeditionary camp siting, development, and maintenance; NBC decontamination; and defensive combat planning and execution. The CSST also deals with military liaison officer/defense attaché officer liaison.

Naval Special Warfare Task Groups and Task Units

Naval Special Warfare Task Groups (NSWTG) and Task Units (NSWTU) are tailored to particular missions and can work independently, jointly, or in combined operations. Their missions include providing command and control elements, and administrative and logistical support.

Special Boat Squadrons (SBR)

These are commanded by Echelon II Captains at NABs Coronado and Little Creek, and provide special operations ships and craft. They comprise one or more active-duty or reserve-component Special Boat Units (SBUs) and Cyclone Class Patrol Coastal (PC) ships.

Special Boat Units (SBUs)

These units are trained and equipped to operate a variety of special operations surface craft in maritime and riverine environments.

SEAL Delivery Vehicle Task Unit

This is comprised of one or more SDV or SEAL platoons, and is led by an SDV Team commanding officer or executive officer. It carries out submersible systems operations from specially configured submarines equipped with Dry Deck Shelters (DDS).

SEAL Platoon

The platoon is commanded by a Navy Lieutenant (O-3), and consists of 16 SEALs. It can be divided into two squads or four elements. All SEALs are qualified in diving, parachuting, and demolition.

Mobile Communications Team

The communications-electronics departments of NSW Groups One and Two provide operational communications in support of NSW forces. They provide new equipment and develop tactics for communications operations and support, and prepare, implement, and review communications plans.

A RHIB being deployed. Their main role is to land and retrieve SEAL forces from enemy-occupied beaches.

NAVAL SPECIAL WARFARE GROUP ONE

Naval Special Warfare Group One (NSWG 1), at Coronado, is one of the six major operational components of Naval Special Warfare Command. Commanded by a Captain (O-6), it has operational and administrative control of SEAL Teams One, Three, Five, and SEAL Delivery Vehicle Team One. It also has administrative control of Naval Special Warfare Unit One (NSWU 1) and Naval Special Warfare Unit Three (NSWU 3). Geographically, NSWG 1 concentrates on the Pacific and Central Commands.

SEAL Team One

SEAL Team One is based at Coronado, and is commanded by a Navy Commander (O-5). It has eight operational SEAL platoons and a headquarters element, and its geographic area of concentration is Southeast Asia. SEAL Team

One deploys platoons to NSWU 1 in Guam and conducts deployments for training (DFTs) throughout the Pacific and Central theaters.

SEAL Team Three

SEAL Team Three is based at Coronado. Led by a Navy Commander (O-5), it has eight operational platoons and a headquarters element. Its geographic area of concentration is Southwest Asia. SEAL Team Three deploys platoons to NSWU 1 in Guam aboard amphibious ships deployed to Seventh, Fifth, and Third Fleets, and conducts DFTs throughout the Pacific and Central Theaters.

SEAL Team Five

SEAL Team Five is based at Coronado, under a Navy Commander (O-5). It has eight operational platoons and a headquarters element. SEAL Team Five's geographic area of concentration is the Northern Pacific, and it deploys platoons to NSWU 1 in Guam, aboard amphibious ships deployed to Seventh, Fifth, and Third Fleets, and conducts DFTs throughout the Pacific and Central Theaters.

SEAL Delivery Vehicle Team One

SEAL Delivery Vehicle Team One (SDVT 1) is based in Pearl Harbor, Hawaii. It is led by a Navy Commander (O-5), and has three operational SEAL Delivery Vehicle (SDV)/Dry Deck Shelter (DDS) Task Units and a headquarters element. Each SDV/DDS Task Unit is designed to operate independently from a host submarine in carrying out NSW missions. SDV/DDS Task Units normally deploy only aboard host submarines, but may be deployed from shore or surface ships. SDVT 1 operates throughout the Pacific and Central Command's geographic areas of responsibility.

Naval Special Warfare Unit One

Naval Special Warfare Unit One (NSWU 1) is based in Guam. Led by a Navy Commander (O-5), it consists of a headquarters element and has operational control of SEAL platoons and Special Boat Unit detachments from NSWG 1 and from Special Boat Squadron One that forward deploy to NSWU 1 on six-month rotation. NSWU 1 maintains operational control of five forward deployed SEAL platoons and two SBU Rigid Hull Inflatable Boat (RHIB) detachments. It is under the administrative command of NSWG 1, but operationally reports to Special Operations Command, Pacific, and US Navy Seventh Fleet for operational tasking. NSWU 1 provides operational support to forward deployed platoons and conducts theater planning for contingencies and exercises for NSW forces in the Pacific. It is capable of forming the nucleus of a Naval Special Warfare Task Unit.

Naval Special Warfare Group One, Detachment Kodiak

Detachment Kodiak is located in Kodiak, Alaska. It is a six-man training cadre that specializes in

Special Warfare Combatant Crewmen (SWCC) assigned to Special Boat Team Twenty-Two (SBT 22) demonstrate the firepower of the new Special Operations Craft-Riverine (SOC-R) while training at the Stennis Space Center, Mississippi, on April 21, 2004. (US Navy photo)

training SEAL platoons and Special Boat Unit detachments in maritime cold weather operations.

Naval Special Warfare Unit Three

Naval Special Warfare Unit Three (NSWU 3), based in Bahrain, is under the administrative control of NSWG 1. Led by an NSW Commander (O-5), it consists of a small headquarters and forms the core of an NSWTU when deployed. It plans, coordinates, and supports the activities of SEAL platoons and SBU detachments deployed to the US Central Command, exclusive of those organic to amphibious-ready groups and carrier battle groups. In view of the maritime character of the area of responsibility and nature of the operations supported, day-to-day operational control is exercised by COMNAVCENT. Operational control may be shifted to Special Operations Command, Central (SOCCENT) when required by operational tasking.

NAVAL SPECIAL WARFARE GROUP TWO

Naval Special Warfare Group Two (NSWG 2) is located in Little Creek, Virginia, and is one of the six major operational components of Naval Special Warfare Command. NSWG 2 is commanded by a Navy Captain (O-6). It has operational and administrative control of SEAL Teams Two, Four, and Eight, SDVT 2, NSWU 4 and NSWU 10. It also has administrative control of NSWU 2 and NSWU 8. Naval Special Warfare Group Two geographically concentrates on the Atlantic, Europe and Southern Command.

SEAL Team Two

SEAL Team Two, based at Little Creek, is commanded by a Navy Commander (O-5). It has eight operational platoons and a headquarters element, and its geographic area of concentration is Europe. SEAL Team Two deploys platoons to NSWU 2 in Germany, aboard amphibious ships deployed to Second and Sixth Fleets, and conducts deployments for training throughout the European theater. It is the only SEAL team with an arctic warfare capability.

SEAL Team Four

SEAL Team Four is based at Little Creek. Under a Navy Commander (O-5), it has ten operational platoons and a headquarters element. SEAL Team Four's geographic area of concentration is Central and South America. It deploys platoons to NSWU 8 in Panama, aboard amphibious ships deployed to Second Fleet, and in support of the annual UNITAS cruise, and conducts DFTs throughout the Central and South American theater. Members of SEAL Team Four speak Spanish; it is the only SEAL team with a viable standing language.

SEAL Team Eight

SEAL Team Eight, based at Little Creek, is under a Navy Commander (O-5). With eight operational platoons and a headquarters element, its geographic area of concentration is the Caribbean,

At sea aboard USS *Mount Whitney* (LCC/JCC 20), January 17, 2003. A SEAL fast-ropes from an MH-53 Pave Low helicopter during a maritime interception operation training exercise. Fast-roping replaced the more traditional insertion method of rappelling, perfected by special forces during the Vietnam War. Fast-roping insertions are the favorite method by which to seize gas and oil platforms.

Africa, and the Mediterranean. SEAL Team Eight deploys platoons with carrier battle groups and amphibious ships in support of Second, Fifth, and Sixth Fleet commanders. It conducts DFTs throughout the Caribbean, Africa, and the Mediterranean.

Naval Special Warfare Unit Two

Naval Special Warfare Unit Two (NSWU 2) is based in Stuttgart, Germany. Commanded by a Navy Commander (O-5), it consists of a headquarters element and has operational SEAL platoons and Special Boat Unit detachments from Naval Special Warfare Group Two and from Special Boat Squadron Two that forward deploy to NSWU 2 on six-month rotation. NSWU 2 maintains operational control of two forward deployed SEAL platoons and a Special Boat Unit RHIB detachment. The unit is under the administrative control of NSWG 2, but operationally reports to Special Operations Command, Europe. NSWU 2 can form the nucleus of a Naval Special Warfare Task Unit.

Naval Special Warfare Unit Four

Naval Special Warfare Unit Four (NSWU 4) is based at Naval Station Roosevelt Roads, Puerto Rico. It is commanded by a Navy Lieutenant Commander (O-4), and consists of a headquarters element and an integrated Special Boat Unit detachment. NSWU 4 is a training command that provides training support to SEAL platoons, SDV Task Units, Special Boat Unit detachments and other special operations forces conducting training in the Puerto Rico operational areas. The unit is under the operational and administrative control of Naval Special Warfare Group Two.

Naval Special Warfare Unit Eight

Naval Special Warfare Unit Eight (NSWU 8) is based in Rodman, Panama, and led by a Navy Commander (O-5). It consists of a headquarters element and has operational SEAL platoons from Naval Special Warfare Group Two that forward deploy to NSWU 8 on six-month rotation. NSWU 8 maintains operational control of two SEAL platoons and Special Boat Unit Twenty-six. The unit is under the administrative control of Naval Special Warfare Group Two, and operational control of Special Operations South and Atlantic Fleet, South. NSWU 8 is capable of forming the nucleus of a Naval Special Warfare Task Unit.

Naval Special Warfare Unit Ten

Naval Special Warfare Unit Ten (NSWU 10) is based at Naval Station Rota, Spain. Commanded by an NSW Commander (O-5), it has three operational SDV Task Units and a headquarters element. It provides tactical training opportunities for NSW forces deployed aboard Sixth Fleet ships during slack periods while on routine deployments, so NSW forces can maintain their perishable skills. The unit is responsible for all NSW exercises conducted in Spain, and is under the operational and administrative command

Staff Sergeant Justin Roberts escorts K-Dog, a Bottle Nose Dolphin belonging to Commander Task Unit (CTU) 55.4.3, in a rigid hull inflatable back to the well deck and holding areas aboard the USS *Gunston Hall* (LSD 44) in the Arabian Gulf during 2003. CTU 55.4.3 is a multi-national team consisting of Naval Special Clearance Team One, Fleet Diving Unit Three from the United Kingdom, Clearance Dive Team from Australia, and the US Navy's Explosive Ordnance Disposal Mobile Units Six and Eight. These units were conducting deep/shallow water mine countermeasure operations to clear shipping lanes for humanitarian relief as part of Operation *Iraqi Freedom.*

Naval Special Warfare forces practice fast-roping on to a MK V Special Operations Craft. Boarding vessels remains a main role for naval commandos.

of Naval Special Warfare Group Two. NSWU 10 closely coordinates with Special Operations Command, Europe.

SEAL Delivery Vehicle Team Two

SEAL Delivery Vehicle Team Two (SDVT 2), based at Little Creek, is under a Navy Commander (O-5) and has three operational SDV/DDS (Dry Deck Shelter) Task Units and a headquarters element. The team conducts operations throughout the Atlantic and Southern, and European command. SDVT 2 places special emphasis on providing the Sixth Fleet commander with an SDV/DDS capability.

SPECIAL BOAT SQUADRON ONE

Special Boat Squadron One (SBR 1), based at Coronado, is one of the six major operational components of Naval Special Warfare Command. It is commanded by a Navy Captain (O-6). It has under its operational and administrative control Special Boat Units Eleven and Twelve, and four Patrol Coastal Class (PC) ships, USS *Hurricane* (PC 3), USS *Monsoon* (PC 4), USS *Squall* (PC 7), and USS *Zephyr* (PC 8). The squadron deploys PCs and Special Boat Unit detachments worldwide. Special Boat Squadron One geographically concentrates on the Pacific and Central areas of responsibility.

Special Boat Unit Twelve

Special Boat Unit Twelve (SBU 12) is based in Coronado, under a Navy Commander (O-5). It consists of a headquarters element and eight Rigid Hull Inflatable Boat (RHIB) detachments. SBU 12 has up to five MK V Special Operations Craft (SOC) detachments. Each detachment normally consists of two boats with crews. SBU 12 supports open water special operations missions for West Coast NSW forces and deploys detachments aboard amphibious ships, to NSWU 1, and on DFTs throughout the Pacific and Central areas of operation. The unit is under the operational and administrative control of Special Boat Squadron One.

SPECIAL BOAT SQUADRON TWO

Special Boat Squadron Two (SBR 2) is based at Little Creek, and is one of the six major operational components of Naval Special Warfare Command. Commanded by a Navy Captain (O-6), it has administrative and operational control over Special Boat Units Twenty and Twenty-Two, and nine Patrol Coastal Class (PC) ships. The PCs under Special Boat Squadron Two are USS *Cyclone* (PC 1), USS *Tempest* (PC 2), USS *Typhoon* (PC 5), USS *Sirocco* (PC 6), USS *Chinook* (PC 9), USS *Firebolt* (PC 10), USS *Whirlwind* (PC 11), USS *Thunderbolt* (PC 12) and USS *Shamal* (PC 13). SBU 26 reports administratively to this squadron. Special Boat Squadron Two geographically concentrates on the Atlantic, Southern and Europe areas of responsibility.

Special Boat Unit Twenty

Special Boat Unit Twenty (SBU 20) is based in Little Creek and is under a Navy Commander (O-5). It consists of a headquarters element and 13 Rigid Hull Inflatable Boat (RHIB) detachments and two MK V

Special Operations Craft (SOC) detachments. It was planned for SBU 20 to have five MK V SOC detachments. Each detachment consists of two boats. The unit supports open water special operations missions for East Coast NSW forces and deploys detachments aboard amphibious ships and to NSWU 2 and NSWU 10. The unit focuses on providing operational support to the European and Atlantic theaters of operations. SBU 20 is under the operational and administrative control of Special Boat Squadron Two.

Part of the SEALs' considerable arsenal is the Desert Patrol Vehicle (DPV). It is basically an off-road racing vehicle, intended for use anywhere a four-wheel-drive vehicle can go, but with additional speed and maneuverability. It can carry a variety of weapons.

Special Boat Unit Twenty-Two

Special Boat Unit Twenty-Two (SBU 22) is based in New Orleans. Under a Navy Commander (O-5), it consists of a headquarters element and two River Patrol Boat (PBR) detachments, two Mini-Armored Troop Carrier (MATC) detachments and two Light Patrol Boat (PBL) detachments. Each detachment normally consists of two boats with crews. SBU 22 is mainly a reserve organization with over 70 percent of the command being naval reservists. It focuses on providing riverine support in Southern and European theaters of operations. The unit is under the operational and administrative control of Special Boat Squadron Two.

Special Boat Unit Twenty-Six

Special Boat Unit Twenty-Six (SBU 26) is based in Rodman, Panama, and consists of a headquarters element and ten Light Patrol Boat (PBL) detachments. Each detachment normally consists of two boats with crews. SBU-26, which is under a Navy Lieutenant Commander (O-4), conducts operations in the riverine environment in support of the Southern commands. The unit is under the operational control of NSWU 8 and under the administrative control of Special Boat Squadron Two.

US Naval Psychological Operations Forces

The US Navy possesses the capability to produce audiovisual products in the Fleet Audiovisual Command, Pacific. The Fleet Tactical Readiness Group (FTRG) provides equipment and technical support for radio broadcasting to civilian populations and broadcast jamming in the AM frequency band. As the unit is not trained to produce psychological operations products, it must be augmented with personnel trained in this field or linguists when necessary. It can be fully operational within 48 hours' notice. Its equipment consists of a 10.6kw AM band broadcast radio transmitter; a broadcast studio van; antenna tuner; two antennas (a pneumatically raised 100ft top-loaded antenna mast and a 500ft wire helium balloon antenna); and a 30kw generator that provides power to the system.

SEALS load their equipment, packed on pallets, on to a truck before a training mission. SEALs carry more equipment than most traditional infantry units and have come under criticism because of it.

US NAVAL SPECIAL OPERATIONS FORCES 2004

Under Commander Naval Special Warfare Group One

Group One training
- Group One Logistics and Support Unit
- Group One Logistics and Support Unit CSST
- Naval Special Warfare Units One (NSWU 1) and Three (NSWU 3)
- SEAL Teams One (ST 1), Three (ST 3), Five (ST 5), and Seven (ST 7)

Commander Naval Special Warfare Group Two

Group Two training
- Group Two Logistics and Support Unit
- Group Two Logistics and Support Unit CSST
- Naval Special Warfare Units Two (NSWU 2), Four (NSWU 4), and Ten (NSWU 10)
- SEAL Teams Two (ST 2), Four (ST 4), Eight (ST 8), and Ten (ST 10)

Commander Naval Special Warfare Group Three
- Special Boat Team Twelve (SBT 12)
- SEAL Delivery Vehicle Team One (SDVT 1)
- SEAL Delivery Vehicle Team One ASDS

Commander Naval Special Warfare Group Four
- Special Boat Teams Twenty (SBT 20), Twenty detachment Caribbean, Twenty-Two (SBT 22), Twenty-Two det. Sacramento
- SEAL Delivery Vehicle Team Two (SDVT 2)

Naval Special Warfare Center
- SDV training detachment Panama City
- Training det. Key West
- Advanced training det. Little Creek
- Det. Hawaii, Yuma, Hurlburt, and Kodiak
- Naval Small Craft Instruction and Technical Training School (NAVSCIATTS)

NAVAL SPECIAL WARFARE WEAPONS SYSTEMS

The *Special Operations Forces Reference Manual* classifies the systems used by NSW personnel:

Patrol Coastal Class Ship

Naval Special Warfare has taken control of 12 of 13 Patrol Coastal (PC) class ships. The main role of the PC class is coastal patrol and interdiction, with a secondary role of NSW support. Primary employment missions include forward presence, monitoring and detection operations, escort operations, non-combatant evacuation, and foreign internal defense.

The PC class operates in low-intensity environments. NSW operational missions include long-range SEAL insertion/extractions, tactical swimmer operations, intelligence collection, operational deception, and coastal/riverine support. PCs will normally operate as a two-boat detachment. This allows enhanced support and facilitates the assignment of one Mobile Support Team (MST) for every two ships. The MST provides technical assistance and maintenance support during mission turnaround.

Design characteristics:
Length: 170ft
Beam: 25ft
Draft: 7.8ft
Displacement: 328.5 tons (full load)
Fuel capacity: 18,000 gallons
Propulsion: four Paxman diesels
   (3,350 horsepower each)
Generators: two Caterpillar (155 kilowatts each)
Steel hull with aluminum superstructure
Commercial sensors and navigation systems
Complement: four officers, 24 enlisted
Detachment: berthing for nine-man SOF/
   law enforcement detachment

Performance criteria:
Maximum speed: 30-plus knots
Cruising speed: 12 knots
Seaworthiness: survive through sea state five
Maximum range: in excess of 3,000nm (two engines at 16 knots)

Armament:
MK38 25mm rapid fire gun
MK96 25mm rapid fire gun
Stinger station
Four pintles supporting any combination of: .50-cal. machine guns;
   M60 machine guns; MK19 grenade launchers
Small arms
MK52 Mod 0 chaff decoy launching system
Pre-planned product improvement: RHIB retrieval system

Members of SEAL Team Two conduct SDV training in the Caribbean, October 2, 1997. SDV units are tasked with a variety of missions, including harbor anti-shipping attacks and hydrographic reconnaissance. The SDV is a "wet" submersible designed to carry combat swimmers and their gear in fully flooded compartments.

MK V Special Operations Craft

The MK V Special Operations Craft (SOC) is the newest craft in the NSW inventory. The MK V SOC's primary role is as a medium-range insertion and extraction platform for special operations forces in a low- to medium-threat environment. Its secondary role is limited coastal patrol and interdiction, specifically limited duration patrol and low- to medium-threat coastal interdiction. The MK V SOC will normally operate in a two-craft detachment with a Mobile Support Team (MST).

The MST provides technical assistance and maintenance support during mission turnaround. The MK V SOC is fundamentally a single-sortie system with a 24-hour turnaround time. The typical MK V SOC mission lasts 12 hours. The MK V SOC is fully interoperable with the

Patrol Coastal (PC) ships and rigid hull inflatables. As such, all could be employed from a forward operating base in a synergistic effect. A MK V SOC detachment, consisting of two craft and support equipment, will be deployable on two USAF C-5 aircraft into the theater within 48 hours of notification. A detachment is transportable over land on existing roadways. Detachments are not configured nor manned to provide their own security, messing, or berthing for personnel while forward deployed.

This clearly demonstrates some of the variety of equipment at the disposal of Naval Special Warfare forces. Here, MK V Special Operations Craft are tied up alongside each other in the Middle East during 2003. On them are Combat Rubber Raiding Craft (CRRC), used for clandestine surface insertion and extraction of lightly armed special operations forces.

Design characteristics:
Length: 81ft 2in.
Beam: 17ft 5³⁄₄ in.
Draft: 5ft
Displacement: 57 tons (full load)
Fuel capacity: 2,600 gallons
Propulsion: two MTU 12V396 diesels (2,285 horsepower each)
Two KaMeWa waterjets
Aluminum hull with five watertight compartments
Radar, full-suite communications (HF, UHF, HF, SATCOM), GPS, IFF
Complement: one officer, five enlisted
Detachment: 16 special operations force combat-loaded personnel
    with four Combat Rubber Raiding Craft (CRRCs)
Performance criteria:
Maximum speed: 45–48 knots for 250nm in sea state two
Cruising speed: 25–40 knots at sea state three
Seaworthiness: survive through sea state five
Maximum range: 500nm (two engines at 45 knots)
Armament:
Stinger station
Five pintles supporting any combination of: .50-cal. machine guns;
    M60 machine guns; MK19 grenade launchers
Small arms
Pre-planned product improvement: mounting stations for
    GAU-17 Minigun; MK95 twin .50-cal. machine gun; MK38
    chain gun
Rolling stock per two-boat detachment:
Two MK V SOC transporters
Two M9161A prime movers
Two M1083 5-ton trucks
Four M1097 HUMMVs with S250 shelters
One 5-ton forklift

River Patrol Boat

The River Patrol Boat (PBR) is designed for high-speed riverine patrols in contested areas of operations, and insertion/extraction of SEAL team elements. More than 500 units were built when first introduced in the Vietnam conflict in 1966, although the current inventory is 24 craft. They can be transported in USAF C-5 aircraft, on skids. The PBR is heavily armed and vital crew areas are protected with ceramic armor. The weapons loadout on this craft includes both single and twin .50-cal. machine gun mounts, 40mm grenade launchers and small arms. The hull is reinforced fiberglass with two Jacuzzi-type waterjet pumps for propulsion. The unit can operate in shallow debris-filled water. The craft is highly maneuverable and can turn 180 degrees and reverse course within its own length while operating at full power. Engine noise silencing techniques have been incorporated into the design and improved over the years. The combination of relatively quiet operation and its surface search radar system make this unit an excellent all-weather picket as well as a shallow-water patrol and interdiction craft.

Design characteristics:
Length: 32ft
Beam (including guard rails): 11ft 7 in.
Weight: $8\frac{3}{4}$ tons
Draft: 2ft
Propulsion: Two GM 6V53N diesel engines
    (215 horsepower each)
Two Jacuzzi 14YJ waterjet pumps
Radar, VHF/UHF radios
Complement: four crew and six passengers
Fiberglass-reinforced hull
Performance characteristics:
Speed: 24 knots
Seaworthiness: sea state three
Maximum range: 300nm at full speed
Armament:
Standard:
Twin mount .50-cal. machine gun
.50-cal. machine gun, stand mounted
MK19 40mm grenade launcher
Options:
40mm/.50-cal. machine gun, stand mounted
60mm mortar
M60 machine guns

Mini-Armored Troop Carrier

The Mini-Armored Troop Carrier (MATC) is a 36ft all-aluminum hull craft designed for high-speed patrol, interdiction, and combat assault missions in rivers, harbors, and protected coastal areas. The MATC has a large well area for transporting combat-equipped troops, carrying cargo, or for gunnery personnel operating the seven organic weapon stations. The MATC propulsion system is similar to that of the River

Rate insignia of Navy Enlisted personnel.

Pay Grade	Rate	Abbreviation	Upper Sleeve	Collar and Cap
E-1	Seaman Recruit	SR		none
E-2	Seaman Apprentice	SA		none
E-3	Seaman	SN		none
E-4	Petty Officer Third Class	PO3		
E-5	Petty Officer Second Class	PO2		
E-6	Petty Officer First Class	PO1		
E-7	Chief Petty Officer	CPO		
E-8	Senior Chief Petty Officer	SCPO		
E-9	Master Chief Petty Officer	MCPO		
E-9	Master Chief Petty Officer of the Navy	MCPON		

19

Pay Grade	Rank	Abbreviation	Collar	Shoulder	Sleeve
O-1	Ensign	ENS			
O-2	Lieutenant Junior Grade	LTJG			
O-3	Lieutenant	LT			
O-4	Lieutenant Commander	LCDR			
O-5	Commander	CDR			
O-6	Captain	CAPT			
O-7	Rear Admiral (lower half)	RDML			
O-8	Rear Admiral (upper half)	RADM			
O-9	Vice Admiral	VADM			
O-10	Admiral	ADM			
O-11	Fleet Admiral*	FADM			

Rate insignia of Navy Commissioned Officers.

Patrol Boat (PBR), with an internal jet pump, which moves the water on the same principle as the air-breathing jet engine. This type of propulsion is especially appropriate for beaching operations. A hydraulic bow ramp is designed to aid the insertion and extraction of troops and equipment. The craft has a low silhouette which makes it difficult to detect in all speed ranges. The unit is extremely quiet, particularly at idle speeds. A high-resolution radar and multiple communications suite provides a good all-weather surveillance and command and control presence for interdiction and anti-smuggling operations. The overhead canopy can be removed or stowed below. Crew size is normally four but can be modified depending on the mission and mission duration.

Design characteristics:
Length: 36ft
Beam (including guard rails): 12ft 9in.
Draft: 2ft
Displacement: 12.5 tons
Propulsion: two GM 8V53N diesel engines
  (283 horsepower each)
Two Jacuzzi 20YJ waterjet pumps
Aluminum hull, flat bottom
Radar, VHF/UHF radios
Complement: four crew and eight passengers

Performance criteria:
Maximum speed: 25-plus knots
Seaworthiness: sea state three
Maximum range: 350nm

Armament:
Seven pintle-mounted weapons to include
.50-cal., M60, MK19
60mm mortar

Light Patrol Boat

The Light Patrol Boat (PBL) is a lightly armed Boston Whaler-type craft with no armor. This craft is constructed of fiberglass with reinforced transom and weapons mount areas. It is powered by dual outboard motors and is highly maneuverable. It is useful in interdicting a lightly armed adversary but should not be used to engage a heavily armed or well-organized enemy. It functions effectively in policing actions, harbor control, diving and surveillance operations, riverine warfare, drug interdiction, and other offensive or defensive purposes.

The weapon mountings can include .50-cal. heavy machine guns or 7.62mm machine guns mounted on 180-degree mounts, providing an effective weapon employment in any direction. Due to its unique hull design, the PBL is excellent for the riverine environment, allowing it to operate in virtually any water depth. Its two low-profile engines are capable of providing eight hours of continuous operation at a fast cruise speed of 25-plus knots. It displaces 6,500lb fully loaded and is transportable via its own trailer, helicopter sling, or C-130 aircraft. Normal crew size is three personnel.

Design characteristics:
Length: 25ft
Max beam: 8ft 7in.
Draft: 18in.
Propulsion: twin 155hp outboards
Fiberglass hull
VHF, UHF, and SATCOM radios
Complement: three crew and eight passengers

Performance criteria:
Speed: 30-plus knots
Range: 150nm
Seaworthiness: sea state two

Armament:
Three weapons stations, one forward and two aft. Combination of .50-cal., or M60

Pay Grade	Rank	Abbreviation	Collar	Shoulder	Sleeve
W-1*	Warrant Officer	WO1			
W-2	Chief Warrant Officer	CWO2			
W-3	Chief Warrant Officer	CWO3			
W-4	Chief Warrant Officer	CWO4			
W-5*	Chief Warrant Officer	CWO5			

Rigid Hull Inflatable Boat

The Rigid Hull Inflatable Boat (RHIB) is a high-speed, high-buoyancy, extreme weather craft whose main role is the insertion/extraction of SEAL tactical elements from enemy occupied beaches. The RHIB is constructed of glass reinforced plastic with an inflatable tube gunwale made of a new hypalon neoprene/nylon reinforced fabric. There are two types of RHIBs currently in the inventory, a 24ft and a 30ft. The RHIB has shown its ability to operate in light-loaded condition in sea state six and winds of 45 knots. For other than heavy-weather coxswain training, operations are limited to sea state five and winds of 34 knots or less. The 24ft version carries a crew of three and a SEAL element. A 30ft craft carries a crew of three and enables SEAL squad delivery.

Rate insignia of Navy Warrant Officers. *The grade of Warrant Officer (W-1) is no longer in use. W-5 was established in the Navy in 2002.

Design characteristics:

	24ft RHIB;	10m RHIB
Length:	24ft	30ft
Beam:	9ft	11ft
Draft:	2ft	3ft
Weight:	9,300lb	14,700lb
Propulsion:	single Volvo Penta	two Iveco diesels with waterjets
Complement:	three crew, four passengers	three crew, eight passengers
Radar:	HF, UHF, VHF	HF, UHF, VHF, SATCOM radios

Performance criteria:

Speed:	25-plus knots	35-plus knots
Range:	170nm	200nm
Seaworthiness:	sea state five	sea state five

Armament:
Forward and after mounts
Mounts   capable of M60   Capable of M60, M2, or MK19

Combat Rubber Raiding Craft

The Combat Rubber Raiding Craft (CRRC) is used for clandestine surface insertion and extraction of lightly armed special operations forces, and capable of over-the-horizon landing and recovery. The CRRC is capable of surf passages. It may be launched from the sea or by airdrop. It may also be deck-launched or locked-out from submarines. It has a low visual electronic signature, and is capable of being cached by its crew once ashore. It uses one 35–55 horsepower engine.
Design characteristics:
Length: 15ft 5in.
Beam: 6ft 3in.
Draft: 2ft
Weight: 265lb without motor or fuel
Speed: 18 knots, no load
Range: dependent on fuel carried
Complement: eight maximum

SEAL Delivery Vehicle MK VIII

The SEAL Delivery Vehicle (SDV) MK VIII is a "wet" submersible, designed to carry combat swimmers and their cargo in fully flooded compartments. Submerged, operators and passengers wear underwater breathing apparatus (UBA). Operations for the vehicle include underwater mapping and terrain exploration, location and recovery of lost or downed objects, reconnaissance work, and limited direct action missions.

The vehicle is propelled by an all-electric propulsion subsystem powered by rechargeable silver-zinc batteries. Buoyancy and pitch attitude are controlled by a ballast and trim system; control in both the horizontal and vertical planes is provided through a manual control stick to the rudder, elevator, and bow planes. A computerized Doppler navigation sonar displays speed, distance, heading, altitude, and other piloting functions. Instruments and other electronics units are housed in dry, watertight canisters. The special modular construction provides easy removal for maintenance. Major subsystems are hull, propulsion, ballast/trim, control, auxiliary life support, navigation, communications, and docking sonar.

Dry Deck Shelter

The Dry Deck Shelter (DDS) allows for the launch and recovery of a SEAL Delivery Vehicle (SDV) or Combat Rubber Raiding Craft (CRRC) with personnel from a submerged submarine. It consists of three modules constructed as one integral unit. The first module is a hangar in which an SDV or CRRC is stowed. The second module is a transfer trunk to allow passage between the modules and the submarine. The third module is a hyperbaric recompression chamber. The DDS provides a dry working environment for mission preparation. In a typical operation the DDS hangar module will be flooded, pressurized to the surrounding sea pressure, and a large door is opened to allow for launch and recovery of the vehicle. A DDS can be transported by USAF C-5/C-17 aircraft, rail, highway, or sealift. The DDS is 40ft long and weighs 65,000lb. Submarines able to use a single DDS are the USS *L. Mendel Rivers* and the USS *Bates*. Submarines capable of dual DDS use are the USS *Kamehameh* and the USS *Polk*.

Design characteristics:
Length: 39ft
Width: 10ft
Weight: 65,000lb
Volume: 3,705 cu ft

Desert Patrol Vehicle

The Desert Patrol Vehicle (DPV) is correctly named the Desert Patrol/Light Strike Vehicle. It is a modified Chenowith off-road, three-man, 2x4 racing vehicle. The DPV was designed to operate anywhere a four-wheel-drive vehicle can, with additional speed and maneuverability.

The DPV can perform numerous combat roles, including special operations; delivery; command and control; weapons platform; rear area combat operations; reconnaissance; forward observation; military police work; and artillery forward observer. The weapon systems used with the DPVs are: Mk19 40mm grenade machine gun, M2 .50-cal. machine gun, M60 7.62 machine gun, AT-4 missile, low-recoil 30mm cannon, and TOW missile launcher.

Vehicle specifications:
Main contractor: Chenowith
Acceleration: 0–30mph in four seconds
Powerplant: 2,000cc gas engine
Maximum speed: 60mph
Payload: 1,500lb
Range: 200-plus miles
Dimensions:
Length: 161in.
Height: 79in.
Width: 83in.
Gross vehicle weight: 2,700lb
Maximum grade: 75 percent
Maximum side slope: 50 percent
Ground clearance: 16in.

Advanced SEAL Delivery System

The Advanced SEAL Delivery System (ASDS) is a dry, mini-submersible that can transport a SEAL squad from a host platform, either surface ship or submarine, to an objective area. The ASDS has a lock-out chamber controlled by operators for lock-out from an anchored position. The ASDS will anchor above the bottom between 2ft and 190ft. The ASDS can be transported by land, sea, or USAF C-5/C-17 aircraft.

Design characteristics:
Length: 65ft
Beam: 6.75ft
Height: 8.25ft
Displacement: 55 tons
Propulsion: 67hp electric motor (Ag-Zn battery)

PERSONAL WEAPONS SYSTEMS
Handguns
Beretta M9 9mm
Colt M1991A1 .45

Heckler & Koch P7M13

9mm SIG Sauer P226

Revolver .357 Magnum S&W

MK23 MOD .45-cal. offensive handgun with suppressor and laser aiming module

Rifles

M16 plus derivatives

Carbine automatic M4A1, 5.56mm

Chicom Type 56 (AK-47)

7.62 M14 semi or automatic rifle

Grenade launchers

40mm, M203

MK19 40mm Mod 3

Mortar

60mm M224

Shotgun

12 GA Mossberg, pump

Remington 870 Wingmaster 12-gauge

Machine guns

MK43 7.62mm

M2HB .50-cal.

Golf 240

Sub-machine gun

MP5 series 9mm

Rockets

M136 anti-tank, AT-4

M72 LAW

M3 Carl Gustaf Recoilless rifle, anti-tank/anti-material rocket assist 84mm

Stinger anti-aircraft missile launcher (FIM-92A)

This is the *raison d'être* of the Navy SEAL. The diver wears Dräger equipment, a German-manufactured closed circuit apparatus intended for use in shallow water where traditional bubble-generating open circuit systems could prove deadly by revealing the diver's presence to an enemy. SEALs used this equipment to destroy a ship during Operation *Just Cause* in Panama, the first time since World War Two that frogmen successfully executed an underwater operation against a vessel.

Sniper weapons
M14 sniper kit and rifle
N91 RH/LH 7.62mm bolt gun, sniper rifle
300 WINMAG bolt gun, sniper rifle
M88 .50-cal. PIP bolt gun, magazine-fed sniper rifle

SCUBA AND UNDERWATER DIVE SYSTEMS
The main focus of SEAL operations, and the reason for the SEALs' very existence, is their ability to function in water. Due to the highly diverse missions modern-day Navy SEALs are expected to undertake, underwater operations are no longer the "bread and butter" work once only associated with frogmen and UDTs. While SEALs currently conduct long-range patrols in land-locked countries such as Afghanistan, other special operations forces practice waterborne operations.

Navy commandos use three main types of underwater breathing apparatus: open circuit compressed air; closed circuit (100 percent pure oxygen) LAR V Dräger underwater breathing apparatus (UBA); and closed circuit (mixed gas) MK15 UBA.

Open circuit systems
Open circuit systems allow air to be breathed from a supply tank and then exhausted directly into the surrounding water. The traditional supply tank(s) can be worn on the diver's back (Scuba). SEAL Delivery Vehicles (SDVs) feature tanks as well, so if the diver is using an SDV he may utilize those tanks instead. As with all dives, deep operation may require diver decompression in conformation with the US Navy standard air decompression table.

Closed circuit oxygen UBA
The LAR V Dräger is a German-manufactured, self-contained, closed circuit and double hosed underwater breathing apparatus that is designed to work exclusively on oxygen, which it recycles after use. Closed circuit systems such as the Dräger are intended for underwater operations in shallow water where traditional bubble-generating open circuit systems could prove deadly. The LAR V is worn on the diver's chest. Numerous factors need to be considered by the user, including depth, rate of work and temperature. Dive teams which used the Dräger in combat in 1989 said that 20ft was considered the safe limit, but that they had dived as deep as 50ft.

Closed circuit mixed gas UBA
The MK 15 is a self-contained, closed circuit, mixed gas, underwater breathing apparatus. The breathing gas is completely retained within the apparatus except during ascent when excess pressure is vented. In the MK 15, oxygen is mixed with a dilutent gas (normally air) to maintain a present partial pressure of oxygen (PPO2) level. The constantly preset PPO2 level allows greater depth and duration than with a 100 percent oxygen system. The duration of the MK 15 is limited by the carbon dioxide scrubber canister. Long duration or deep dives may require diver decompression in accordance with US Navy decompression tables.

NAVY SEALS AT WAR:
OPERATION *URGENT FURY*

On October 25, 1983, the United States invaded the small Caribbean island of Grenada. The US viewed the ever-increasing presence of Cuban workers and advisers as a threat to her hegemony over the region and invaded under the pretext that American students were in harm's way as civil war was threatening to erupt.

Navy SEALs conducted four missions during the invasion: the reconnaissance of Point Salines airfield and emplacement of navigational beacons there; the special reconnaissance of Pearls airfield; the assault on the Radio Free Grenada transmitting station; and the assault and hostage rescue at the Governor General's mansion.

POINT SALINES AIRFIELD RECONNAISSANCE AND BEACON EMPLACEMENT

The SEALs were tasked with two missions on October 23. The first was to acquire timely intelligence on Point Salines airfield. This included a reconnaissance of the airfield tarmac to find out if it was free of any debris or obstacles that could impede the American forces whose job was to seize it. The other was to place navigational beacons to help guide US aircraft carrying two under-strength battalions of the 75th Infantry (Rangers) whose primary mission was to carry out a parachute assault on the airfield, seize it, and secure it.

Sixteen members of SEAL Team Six were aboard two MC 130 E Combat Talons, each of which carried a 25ft fiberglass Light Patrol Boat. Team Six, which was based at Dam Neck, Virginia, was the US Navy's crack anti-terrorist unit, numbering fewer than 180 personnel. The SEALs were set to conduct a combat waterborne parachute drop, get into their Boston Whalers and rendezvous with the USS *Clifton Sprague* where the commandos would link up with three additional SEALs and three combat controllers from the Air Force. From that point on the combined special operations team would infiltrate the surrounding beach areas with their boats and carry out their primary mission.

Intelligence at Grenada was spartan at best. Accurate maps did not exist and there hadn't been enough time for proper planning. Initial plans included deploying from a submarine, but, as Major Mark Adkin explained in *Urgent Fury; The Battle for Grenada*, the SEALs in Puerto Rico had not yet been trained to properly deploy from that particular submarine. What would have been considered a standard naval commando infiltration, the insertion of frogmen via submarine, was null and void due to a training

Naval Special Warfare forces with fins attached prepare to conduct a water jump. Waterborne parachuting can be extremely hazardous and led to the deaths of four Navy SEALs during the invasion of Grenada in 1983.

shortfall. Therefore, the operation shifted to the waterborne method via parachute jump. This is risky, no matter what sort of conditions it is conducted under. Heavy gear and the unpredictability of the ocean would surely have made this one of the most hazardous ways of getting the SEALs in. As is typical with many special operations forces in combat, rucksacks are overloaded with heavier live ammunition (blank training rounds weigh much less) and other mission-essential war materiel.

The excess gear and equipment, partly the byproduct of the certain sense of invincibility not uncommon in elite troops, had tragic results for some of the men. Despite the recommended weight being no more than 60lbs, the average SEAL probably carried more than 100lbs for the jump. This phenomenon of packing more than necessary also has its roots in the fact that, like all special operations forces, SEALs tend to be lightly armed and have to be able to sustain a fire-fight when compromised. Another factor was probably that the Grenadian forces, the People's Revolutionary Army (PRA), around the objective at Point Salines had mechanized units equipped with BTR 60 armored personnel carriers and BRDMs equipped with 12.7mm anti-aircraft cannons. The PRA numbered around 5,000 troops. An encounter with any part of such a force could prove fatal if the commandos did not have enough fire power to handle the possible contact.

Although the operation was scheduled to take place during dusk, a delay forced the men into a night-time jump. Undoubtedly, the excess weight was a handicap. More importantly, weather conditions had deteriorated. The surface wind at sea level was about 25 knots, whereas 18-knot gusts were considered the limit for a combat jump. The MC 130s flew below radar at 600ft until they approached the insertion point. The aircraft climbed to 2,000ft and, after each aircraft had unloaded its Boston Whaler, the SEALs jumped into the night.

The standard operating procedure for waterborne jumps requires that the paratrooper loosen his parachute harness as he nears the water. This allows him to get clear of the canopy that can easily entangle and snare him. In effect, the paratrooper nearly jumps out of his harness. This is a tricky maneuver and must be practiced regularly. The darkness added to the difficulty of a task where timing is everything. That, along with the unpredictability of the water and the weight of the equipment the men were carrying, led to the deaths of four Navy SEALs. The eight men from the first plane lost three members and had to survive in the open sea until they were picked up by the *Clifton Sprague*. The second team, which lost one man, got on to their boat and made rendezvous with the ship. After linking up, the teams, accompanied by their Air Force controllers, headed for the beach.

A Grenadian patrol boat forced the commandos to retreat. Undeterred, they attempted to infiltrate the area the next night, October 24, but once again encountered an enemy vessel. The SEALs cut their engine and waited. Unable to restart it the men drifted helplessly out to sea where they were picked up 11 hours later by the *Clifton Sprague*.

The mission for the Navy SEALs of Team Six had ended in utter failure. Everything that could go wrong did. The airborne Rangers would capture the airfield at Point Salines without any accurate intelligence or navigational aid.

PEARLS AIRFIELD RECONNAISSANCE

Members of SEAL Team Four, which attached to the 22nd Marine Amphibious Unit (MAU), were tasked with a reconnaissance of the coastline and the airport at Pearls on the northeastern side of Grenada on October 25, in advance of a possible amphibious assault by the Marines. The insertion was conducted with two Seafoxes, low profiled and high-speed boats that carried .50-cal. heavy machine guns and 40mm grenade launchers. The boats were part of Special Boat Unit Twenty.

Aboard USS *Oscar Austin* (DDG 79), October 29, 2002. US Navy SEALs from Little Creek, Virginia, fast-rope on to the fantail of the guided missile destroyer, which was on exercise with the USS *Harry S. Truman* battle group.

Subsequent reconnaissance work along the coastline revealed potential dangers for an amphibious assault and the Marines launched a heliborne attack instead. Other SEALs located a 23mm anti-aircraft gun that would be eliminated during the assault by a Cobra gunship. It was said that the information obtained by the SEALs was not used by the assault forces, and if that was indeed the case it only highlighted the need for a joint special operations command. This command was created three years later to address some of the communications issues.

Overall, the mission was successful and true to the nature of the original purpose of the US Navy SEALs: to conduct clandestine operations in maritime and riverine environments.

RADIO FREE GRENADA TRANSMITTING STATION

Eight SEALs from Team Six on board a Black Hawk helicopter were tasked to seize and hold a Soviet-built radio transmitting station at Beausejour on the west coast of Grenada on October 24–25. The intention was to prevent the PRA communicating with the civilian population; they had earlier broadcast the news of the American invasion. The SEALs were then to wait for an American relief force. The radio station could then be used by US forces to broadcast information to the local population.

As with most of the operations during *Urgent Fury*, few details existed on enemy troop disposition and strength. Detailed maps of the particular region were not available. Logistical delays meant that the element of surprise was lost. Nonetheless, the eight men went in and secured their objective.

Two security elements were then sent out to engage any enemy reaction forces. Two men secured the road to the north while two others situated themselves along the southern route. They were armed with M60 machine guns and M72 light anti-tank weapons. Soon a PRA truck was successfully ambushed to the north, and five enemy soldiers were killed. Not long after a PRA reaction force, led by a BTR 60, advanced from Fort Frederick to the south, and the SEAL element engaged it near a bridge. PRA soldiers tried to flank the American position while the armored personnel carrier pinned down the commandos. An experimental rocket, the 66mm RAW, may have been used to destroy the vehicle. Unable to sustain long periods of contact and having no air support to suppress the Grenadians, the SEALs decided to withdraw. The PRA recaptured the transmitting station as the SEALs fought their way through to the beach where they hid in a well-camouflaged site. After another short engagement, the commandos escaped out to sea. Subsequent air strikes launched from the carrier USS *Independence* and an artillery bombardment from the USS *Caron* failed to topple the transmitting mast.

ASSAULT ON THE GOVERNOR GENERAL'S MANSION

The last SEAL mission during Operation *Urgent Fury* took place simultaneously to the transmitter raid. Two Black Hawks with 23 commandos from SEAL Team Six were assigned to launch an assault on the British Governor General's mansion near St George on the west coast of Grenada. The Governor General, Paul Scoon, was under house arrest along with his staff.

The assault began late and ran straight into trouble when the men were unable to locate the residence due to the density of vegetation, which in turn camouflaged known points. Enemy small arms fire greeted the special forces, but they were soon able to identify their objective. Both elements successfully executed a 90ft fast-rope insertion.

A SEAL team member provides security from a rooftop as part of a non-combatant evacuation exercise at Naval Air Station, Fallon, Nevada, on August 7, 2003. The exercise simulated the rescue of downed aircrew behind enemy lines, enabling other aircrews to perform Combat Search and Rescue (CSAR)-related missions as well as experiment with new techniques in realistic scenarios.

However, one Navy SEAL officer, three State Department officials and the only satellite radio available to communicate with headquarters on the USS *Guam* were left with the helicopters as small arms fire forced the aircraft to hurriedly withdraw.

The remaining 22 SEALs successfully overwhelmed a few local police officers, secured the staff and the Governor General, and consolidated their position. Air evacuation proved impossible due to the increasing ground fire. Soon the commandos were surrounded by the PRA as a BTR 60 attempted to punch through the main gate. Although the PRA attack was driven off, it became clear that immediate assistance was needed. Isolated and without the satellite radio, the SEALs still managed to communicate with higher command, and two Marine Corps Cobra gunships came to their aid. Both Cobras were shot down by hostile fire. Subsequently, and from a greater distance, AC 130 gunships started to create a ring of steel around the beleaguered Americans. For over four hours, Spectre gunships would rotate and remain on station, and by night Navy A7 attack aircraft from the *Independence* flew in support of the SEALs. Finally, on October 26, units from the 22nd Marine Amphibious Unit relieved the commandos.

OPERATION *JUST CAUSE*

A highly sophisticated multi-story kill house in the Persian Gulf region used by special operations forces for close-quarters training.

On December 20, 1989, the United States invaded Panama in a bid to oust her unco-operative leader Manuel Noriega. Locally stationed units as well as troops from the continental US launched numerous missions for control of the country and to locate and capture Noriega. Twenty-seven thousand Americans were involved in the campaign.

As part of Task Force White, Naval Special Warfare Group Two deployed 707 sailors for the military operation in Panama. Navy SEALs were tasked with several missions with the aim of intercepting or destroying any potential escape routes or methods. Three primary missions included the shut-down of the harbor of Colon, the destruction of the boat *Presidente Porres*, which was docked at the pier in Balboa Harbor, and the seizure and destruction of a Lear jet at Patilla airport. Colon's harbor was successfully patrolled by NSW forces, and the vessel was destroyed with precision befitting a Swiss clock as four frogmen from SEAL Team Two penetrated enemy controlled areas and attached underwater explosives, using Dräger rebreathers so as to avoid creating bubbles and thus remain unobserved by Panamanian forces. One member of the team provided this account of the action in Joel Nadel's *Special Men and Special Missions*:

"On the night of December 19, 1989, I was one of four divers from a SEAL Team who was inserted into the waters of the Panama Canal. Our mission was to attach huge sacks of plastic explosives to the hull of... an armed 65ft coastal patrol boat that belonged to the Panamanian Navy, and was to be used as a means of escape for General Noriega. We used an oxygen rebreather, which allowed us to remain submerged for over three hours without making any bubbles. We successfully completed infiltration to the target and secured our charges to the hull and continued on to the extraction location. At exactly 0100hrs on December 20, at a time preset by us before entering the water, the charges detonated and the vessel sank beneath the waters of Balboa Harbor. Throughout the mission, we had to react to numerous situations, which forced us to use all the tricks of the trade from years of combat-proven training. During emplacement of the charges, several fire fights on shore broke out, resulting in a series of underwater explosions in close proximity to us. While there is nothing a diver can do about underwater explosions, except try to avoid them, our level of training allowed us to continue the mission, uninterrupted. Next, while en route to the extraction location, a freighter making its way up the canal forced us to dive to a depth of over 50ft in order to avoid being run over. That exposed us to a different type of threat since pure oxygen can be toxic at depths greater than 20ft. It was instantly apparent that our emphasis on the highest possible physical fitness standards was about to pay off. Our mission lasted about four hours and was the exact type of mission SEALs train for every day."

One thing the account does not mention is that this was the first time since World War Two that frogmen successfully executed an underwater operation against a vessel. This mission is considered a classic in naval commando history.

The attempt to seize or destroy the President's personal jet at the private airport at Patilla was hardly a classic in naval commando operations. Primary intelligence indicated that the private airport was patrolled only by lightly armed civilian guards. No Panamanian regular forces were said to be present. Although the SEALs did rehearse for this mission as well as send out small reconnaissance teams in civilian gear, the overall operation was probably more akin to mission-specific tasks handled by Marine Corps Raider companies or Army Rangers. Arguments can be made that the Rangers were busy seizing the airfields at Rio Hato and Tocumen-Torrijos. Nonetheless, as the United States Special Operations Command (USSOCOM) was newly founded and mostly an Army show, jealousies and inter-service rivalries interfered in sound decision making. For whatever military or political reason, and despite some opposition, the mission was assigned to NAVSPECWAR.

Around midnight a US Navy patrol boat launched 15 Zodiac rubber boats filled with three platoons of 48 SEALs from SEAL Team Four and one Air Force Combat Control Team (AFCCT) member who would coordinate aerial support from a Spectre gunship. Due to a radio message indicating that a helicopter had left Colon with Noriega and was possibly en route to Patilla airport, the raid was launched 15 minutes earlier than planned. The SEAL platoons rushed forward without adequate reconnaissance of the beach area near the airport. Their daring movement proved to be opportune as the beach was empty, but the increased haste of attack didn't help. Panamanian guards yelled out warnings that were met by the American commandos' calls for them to surrender. This stalemate lasted for a short while until hostile fire raked the advancing SEALs. The sudden gunfire and illumination exposed a squad of the Navy frogmen. Seven out of nine were hit almost immediately, as the second section rushed forward to support their mates.

A short and brisk fire-fight echoed throughout the airport, during which an American rocket punched a hole into Noriega's jet. The AFCCT was not able to communicate effectively with air support. Eventually, the fighting ceased, leaving four Navy SEALs dead and an additional eight wounded. Soon Army troops and Rangers relieved their Navy counterparts. The Patilla mission, although successful, was a stark reminder yet again of the vulnerability of special operations forces once unmasked. Lightly armed with no aerial support, the commandos were easily held at bay by a para-military force. Raids in urban areas do depend on surprise, shock, and speed – but just as importantly, they depend on air support once compromised.

Several discussions have taken place regarding this particular attack. One argument reasoned that constricting rules of engagement imposed by higher command made it difficult for the commandos to kill any of the civilian guards, and thus the stalemate led to the deaths of the sailors. Another point is that the SEALs were woefully undermanned to even conduct such a mission. Several "old hands" did object that the airfield raid was not a naval commando mission and should never have been executed. In the end, none of these arguments matters. A hurried plan to send "trigger-pullers" to eliminate one aircraft seems wasteful. A less complicated and possibly easier mission might have been to have eyes on the target with aerial support on stand-by.

Undoubtedly many facts remain unavailable and thus most discussion is hypothetical at best. The one genuine mistake of the mission was that the SEALs were not ready for a fire-fight in terms of basic infantry tactics – supporting fire from the other squads and cover. Too many commandos were caught in the open and were mowed down within seconds before the rest of the platoons could react. Nonetheless, the mission was a success and that is a tribute to the men on the ground.

The Arabian Sea, December 6, 2001. An SH-60F Seahawk helicopter leaves the deck of MV *Kota Sejarah* after dropping off US Navy SEALs and Marines during a search for illegal contraband and al-Qaeda troops. The SPECWAR personnel were deployed aboard the amphibious warfare ship USS *Shreveport* (LPD 12) in support of Operation *Enduring Freedom*. The ship was released following the inspection.

German special forces in Afghanistan, 2002. These elite troops gained an excellent reputation working alongside other Coalition special operations forces. Although they had participated in hostage rescue missions, this was the first time German forces had participated in combat missions since World War Two.

VBSS (VISIT BOARD SEARCH SEIZURE)

On Thursday, February 3, 2000, the Pentagon released evidence of oil smuggling by the Russian tanker *Volgoneft-147*. A US Navy cruiser had intercepted the tanker outside the Persian Gulf the day before but the Russians wouldn't stop. In a normal boarding procedure the Navy vessel comes alongside the other ship. A handful of Navy SEALs from SEAL Team Two fast-roped from a helicopter on to the ship when the Russian vessel refused to yield.

Global positioning satellite logs aboard the *Volgoneft-147* indicated that it had been at the forbidden oil port of Shatt al Arab, in southern Iraq. The US had been tracking the vessel and a second Russian oil tanker for a month with spy satellites, ships, and surveillance aircraft.

OPERATION *ENDURING FREEDOM*

In response to guerrilla attacks launched against the United States on September 11, 2001, SOCOM immediately launched several teams from their special operations arsenal into the Gulf region in preparation to combat the group held responsible for these attacks, al-Qaeda and their hosts the Taliban government of Afghanistan. Contrary to the original role of the Navy SEALs, that is to operate within the riverine and maritime environments, units were deployed to land-locked Afghanistan. Their presence bore a simple explanation – the naval commandos formed part of Task Force K-Bar, a Combined Joint Special Operations Task Force (CJSOTF) South. For the first time, a Navy SEAL captain was responsible for all special operations under the US Central Command. The task force included special operations forces from the United States and other Coalition forces. The CJSOTF consisted of US special forces, SEAL platoons from Teams Two, Three, Eight, and SDV 1; the 4th Psychological Operations Group; Navy Explosive Ordnance Disposal (EOD); Air Force special operations forces; and US Marine Corps CH-53

(continued on page 41)

US NAVY SEALS 1983–2004

A

OPERATION *URGENT FURY*, GRENADA

ZODIAK OPERATIONS CHINOOK

c

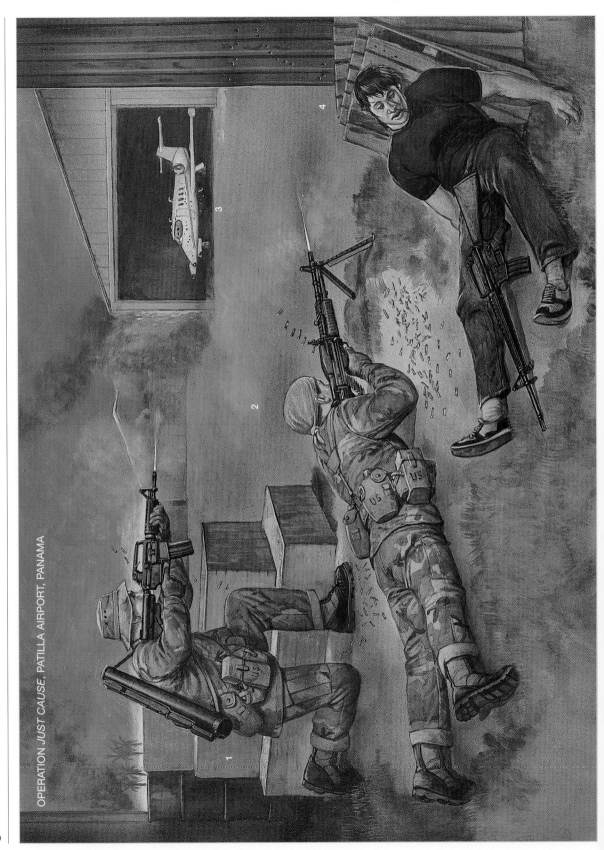

OPERATION *JUST CAUSE*, PATILLA AIRPORT, PANAMA

D

OPERATION *ENDURING FREEDOM*, AFGHANISTAN

1

2

3

4

5

6

E

F

OPERATION *IRAQI FREEDOM*

and TF 160 helicopters. Foreign special forces were also involved – Danish (102 personnel), German Kommando Spezialkräfte(103), Canadian Joint Task Force-2 (40), New Zealand Special Air Service (40), Norwegian Jäger Kommando (50) as well as Marine Jäger Kommando (28), Australian SAS (95), and one special operations forces liaison officer from Turkey. Some of the operations conducted in 2001–02 are summarized with more detailed operations below: 42 strategic reconnaissance missions, 23 direct action missions, 12 underway ship takedowns, and 147 calls for close-air-support fire.

Navy records also reveal that:
"Capt. Robert Harward, commander of San Diego's Naval Special Warfare Group One (CNSWG 1), was awarded Germany's 2nd highest military medal, the Silver Cross of Honor, for his actions as the Commander of Combined Joint Special Operations South Afghanistan (Task Force K-Bar). While other Navy SEAL and SOF units assisted Afghan forces in removing the Taliban government from power, TF K-Bar commandos primarily waged the war on terrorism by destroying the al-Qaeda infrastructure in Afghanistan and disrupting its ability to conduct terrorist operations. During searches of cave and village enclaves in Southern and Eastern Afghanistan, TF K-BAR coalition forces collected valuable intelligence and captured suspected al-Qaeda and Taliban prisoners while conducting combat operations. TF K-Bar forces also orchestrated extensive strategic reconnaissance, conducted Combat Search and Rescue (CSAR), and performed at-sea Leadership Interdiction Operations (LIO) in the search for terrorists trying to escape by ship. In addition to working extensively with US Navy SEALs in Afghanistan, German forces were engaged in combat operations for the first time since World War II."

The primary missions in Afghanistan included reconnaissance and enemy combatant interdiction. SEALs performed SSE (Sensitive Site

Task Force K-BAR in Afghanistan during Operation *Enduring Freedom*. This ultra elite task force was composed of Coalition special operations units tasked with the destruction of senior al-Qaeda and Taliban leaders and infrastructure.

An enormous supply of ammunition and explosives is destroyed by Navy Explosive Ordnance Disposal personnel in Afghanistan, 2002.

Exploitation) missions, such as cave and house searches. Though not specifically tasked with the destruction of enemy weapons and explosives, the abundant war materiel found in Afghanistan made it a natural part of operations for the SEALs. A cave complex assault originally intended as a nine-hour operation actually lasted for up to 10 days.

Meanwhile, a raid on Tarnak Farms resulted in the site being seized, searched, then used as a venue for training. Navy SEAL Chief Petty Officer Matthew Bourgeois was killed here when he stepped on a landmine while conducting breaching training on March 28, 2002. Another raid was conducted after several teams were unable to insert, and resulted in 16 enemy killed and 27 taken prisoner. Special forces also captured cell phones, laptop computers, and PRC-117 radios.

The Department of Defense said that at least seven separate platoons from SEAL Teams Two, Three, Eight and DevGroup (ST 6) as well as elements of SEAL Delivery Vehicle Team One deployed to Afghanistan. Some operated in Pakistan, conducting reconnaissance missions for a potential amphibious invasion, including hydrographic surveying and route and airfield surveys. Visit Board Search Seizure (VBSS) missions were also carried out, to ensure no weapons were being smuggled towards Afghanistan by sea.

Members of SEAL Team Three were inserted covertly into Afghanistan and, for four days prior to the Marines landing at it, observed the small airfield that would later become Camp Rhino. Performing traditional pathfinder missions, the SEALs provided security and marked the landing zone for larger conventional forces. SEALs also jointly operated with members of Delta, the US Army's 1st SFO (D), as part of Task Force 11. The primary mission of this ultra-secret task force was to locate, capture or kill senior members of the Taliban government and al-Qaeda operatives.

In January 2002, an intelligence-gathering mission at Zhawar Kili in eastern Afghanistan, near the Pakistan border, revealed one million lbs of ammunition and equipment hidden within an extensive network of seventy caves and tunnels. Although often touted as an extremely successful mission, the cave complexes at Zhawar Kili are more or less considered a tourist spot by veteran hands familiar with Afghanistan's struggle against the Soviets. During the war against the Soviet Union from 1979 to 1989, American and other foreign political leaders were often shown the enormous and well-constructed caves that housed classrooms, a hospital, and living quarters, by the Afghan mujahedeen in an effort to win financial, political, and military support for their struggle against the invaders. The Soviets fought several unsuccessful engagements in the area.

The SEALs, supported by a reinforced platoon of about 50 Marines charged with providing additional security, explored the caves. Precision-guided munitions were called in to help destroy the entrances. Photographic evidence suggests that these smart bombs severely damaged the cave entrances but ultimately these cave closures

Navy SEALs receive tactical mobility training from Naval Special Warfare Group Two Training Detachment (NSWG 2 TRADET), on August 20, 2003. NSWG 2 TRADET trains all the east coast SEAL teams before they deploy to support missions throughout the world.
(US Navy photo)

are temporary at best. The historical pattern indicates that Afghans have not only patience but that the country is dotted with enormous natural caves.

SEALs, working alongside Danish special forces, captured a key Taliban member, Mullah Khairullah Kahirkhawa, in February 2002. A public relations document reveals that: "Operators of a Predator reconnaissance vehicle orbiting the hills in the Paktia province had seen the Mullah leave a building and radioed the headquarters at Camp Rhino. SEALs and Danish commandos quickly loaded a US Air Force MH-53M Pave Low and headed out within fifteen minutes with an Army AH-64A Apache as escort. An hour and a half after the first notice, the Mullah was on the ground in US custody."

The Battle of Takur Ghar

On March 4, 2002, the largest special operations battle in Afghanistan took place on a mountaintop overlooking the Shah-e-Kot valley in southeastern Afghanistan, called Takur Ghar. As part of Operation *Anaconda*, a Coalition drive that attempted to ensnare well-established Taliban and al-Qaeda fighters in the region, special operations teams were used as the eyes and ears for the conventional army. Up until this point, the war in Afghanistan had been conducted primarily by special operations units. *Anaconda* marked a shift in the war strategy to a more traditional focus.

The one-day fight caused the greatest number of US special operations forces casualties during *Enduring Freedom* thus far. US special operations forces had spent the month monitoring pockets of enemy forces in the valley, southeast of Gardez. In February, the headquarters for US ground forces in Afghanistan, Task Force Mountain, commanded by Major General Franklin L. Hagenback, conceived a classic military "hammer and anvil" maneuver to eliminate the enemy personnel. In the western part of the Shah-e-Kot valley, US troops and Afghan forces in Gardez would push from the west in an effort to clear an area of reported high concentrations of al-Qaeda. This was the hammer. *Anaconda* planners believed this maneuver would force the enemy to flee east into the blocking positions, the anvil, of awaiting American soldiers from the 10th Mountain and 101st Airborne divisions.

LEFT **Some of the cache of ammunition and weapons discovered during a reconnaissance mission in Zhawar Kili, Afghanistan. Note the well-constructed tunnel. One particular assault on part of the country's extensive cave systems was expected to last between nine and ten hours, but went on for up to ten days. Although smart bombs have been used to destroy the entrances to many caves, closing them might turn out to be temporary.**

RIGHT **Another picture taken by SEALs during exploration of the tunnel systems in Zhawar Kili. At one time a section of Afghanistan's massive cave system housed classrooms, a hospital, and living quarters.**

SEALs in classic woodland pattern battledress uniforms with Hechler & Koch MP5s.

Augmenting the conventional forces were small reconnaissance teams. These were drawn from US and Coalition special operations forces and included Navy SEALs, Army special forces and Air Force special tactics operators. These reconnaissance teams were positioned at strategic locations where they established observation posts, provided information on enemy movements, and directed air strikes. These actions resulted in the deaths of hundreds of al-Qaeda and Taliban fighters.

The battle of Takur Ghar began rather inconspicuously as a number of additional Coalition special operations teams were dropped off on various hilltops to provide reconnaissance and call-for-fire support missions during *Anaconda*'s shaky opening moves. One of the unexpected problems encountered by Task Force Mountain was the surprisingly well-disciplined and organized resistance of the guerrillas. Intelligence should have uncovered this prior to the engagement but a hasty invasion of Afghanistan post-September 11, 2001, and the swift collapse of the Taliban regime, may have led to a gross underestimation of the opposition forces. Instead of the eagerly anticipated retreat, the Taliban and al-Qaeda fighters stood their ground, fought and, throughout *Anaconda*, received reinforcements from neighboring groups. These engagements were fought mostly along a number of draws and trails at the southern end of the valley near Marzak, dubbed the "ratline." The unexpected resistance forced regular Afghan forces to withdraw.

Their original objective had been to push east toward "the Whale," a distinctive terrain feature southeast of Gardez. From these hilltops special operations forces had interdicted enemy combatants. The small teams had proven in the past, and in particular during this operation, the extreme effectiveness of their missions – to observe, destroy, and relay crucial intelligence to higher headquarters. The call-for-fire missions were regularly monitored via satellite feeds at headquarters on television and the shows became known as "Kill TV."

The stiff resistance coupled with bad weather conditions made it impossible for Task Force Mountain to deploy all its troops. Lacking the manpower and given the extremely difficult terrain in Afghanistan, the Coalition forces came under extreme duress. During this time the special operations forces teams provided excellent support for the troops pinned down by calling in air strikes and locations of enemy troops and movements. This allowed Maj. Gen. Hagenback to reposition his soldiers to the northern end of the Shah-e-Kot valley and subsequently attack al-Qaeda from there. As the operation unfolded, Task Force Mountain needed more reconnaissance teams in the area. It was during one of the insertion attempts of a small reconnaissance team that the events were triggered that led to an ever-growing

A member of SEAL Team Three clears the entrance to one of the numerous natural caves found throughout Afghanistan.

Navy SEALs secure a US Embassy during a Non-Combatant Evacuation exercise at Fallon Naval Air Station, Nevada, as part of Desert Rescue XI, on August 7, 2003. Desert Rescue XI was a joint service Combat Search and Rescue (CSAR) training exercise hosted by the Naval Strike and Warfare Center at Fallon. The exercise simulated downed aircrew behind enemy lines, enabling other aircrew to perform CSAR-related missions as well as experiment with new techniques in realistic scenarios. (US Air Force photo)

Members of a SEAL team conducting combat operations in Afghanistan, 2002.

avalanche of troops, aircraft, and destruction fed into the maelstrom whirling around the snow-covered mountaintop of Takur Ghar.

One of the teams was made up of SEALs from Dam Neck, Virginia. Their objective was to insert into a 10,000ft, snow-capped mountain which provided first-rate visibility on to the southern approaches of the valley, the "Whale" and Marzak. Thus Takur Ghar had everything required for a perfect site. Unbeknown to the Coalition planners, Taliban and al-Qaeda militia had already seized the hill for the very same reasons some time before. The terrain helped to conceal these forces and, although usually lightly armed, they had rocket-propelled grenades and at least one heavy machine gun positioned well enough to cause problems to any low-flying aircraft.

In the early morning hours of March 4, 2002, al-Qaeda fighters fired on an MH-47E Chinook helicopter carrying a special operations forces reconnaissance element. This resulted in Navy SEAL Aviation Boatswain's Mate (Handling) 1st Class (ABH1) Neil Roberts falling out of the helicopter. Thus began a chain of events culminating in one of the most intense small-unit fire-fights of the war; the deaths of all the al-Qaeda defending the mountaintop; and also in the deaths of seven US servicemen.

As planners for *Anaconda* requested additional reconnaissance teams, plans for insertions were drawn up by March 2 and two teams were to be inserted on different mountains to establish observation posts the following night. Late the following evening two MH-47Es from the 2nd Battalion, 160th Special Operations Aviation Regiment (Airborne), nick-named Night Stalkers, would depart and insert the teams. Razor 04 would emplace a team to the north while the other, Razor 03, carrying Navy SEAL Roberts' team, would deploy SEALs and an Air Force combat controller (CCT) on Takur Ghar.

At approximately 0300hrs on March 4, Razor 03 approached its Helicopter Landing Zone (HLZ) in a small saddle atop Takur Ghar. It is standard operating procedure to overfly the intended landing zone prior to insertion. One of the pilots in an after-action report stated that a C-130 may have conducted an aerial reconnaissance over Takur Ghar. Whether or not a manned or unmanned craft conducted the overflight, one thing is for

Navy SEALs verify the identity of individuals during a Non-Combatant Evacuation training exercise as part of Desert Rescue XI, on August 7, 2003. Desert Rescue XI was a joint service Combat Search and Rescue (CSAR) training exercise at Fallon Naval Air Station, Nevada. (US Air Force photo)

The enormous amount of equipment required to sustain a small team in a hostile environment. This vehicle features an MK40 grenade launcher.

certain – it was dotted with tracks. A slight delay was caused by a B-52 strike in the vicinity in support of *Anaconda*, and maintenance problems with a helicopter. The original HLZ was changed to another.

As Razor 03 approached, both the pilots and the men in the back observed fresh tracks in the snow, goatskins, and other signs of recent human activity. As discussions took place between the pilots and the team, a shoulder-launched RPG round hit the large helicopter. Small arms fire peppered the craft. One man was wounded immediately and Razor 03's hydraulic and oil lines were shredded. Immediate evasive actions by the pilot caused two men to fall out of the open ramp of the helicopter. One of the crewmen was tethered while Navy SEAL Roberts was not. Whether or not the helicopter was in the process of setting down is not clearly established but certainly Roberts must have fallen at least five if not 15ft to the ground. As the Chinook lurched off the mountaintop the SEAL was on his own, surrounded by at least half a dozen fighters.

As there was no ongoing surveillance at the time, the circumstances of Roberts' death are primarily based on conjecture and forensic evidence. The Department of Defense's official conclusion is that "Roberts survived the short fall from the helicopter, likely activated his signaling device, and engaged the enemy with his squad automatic weapon. He was mortally injured by gunfire as they closed in on him."

Roberts, 32, was a 14-year Navy veteran, and the first Navy SEAL and the first sailor killed in action during Operation *Enduring Freedom*. One can only imagine what transpired during those few moments; undoubtedly some of the training took over as well as survival instincts. The "pucker-factor" (tension level) was probably very high as he realized his only help was leaving, struggling not to crash. After the battle emails flooded the internet with stories of

Roberts' extreme heroism and calls for the Medal of Honor as he supposedly had wiped out numerous enemy fighters and at least one machine gun nest. The Department of Defense's account clearly denies this, but the most important consideration should be that even exceedingly well-trained men and well-laid plans can and will fall victim to Murphy's Law; that what can go wrong, will go wrong. Navy SEAL Roberts did what he could given the impossible scenario unfolding around him.

Back at the controls of Razor 03, the pilots managed to execute a crash-landing some seven kilometers north of where Roberts had fallen out. Accountability is always stressed in the military, and a quick head-count revealed the absence of one of their own. The mood must have been unbearable: the men surely felt a variety of emotions as they contemplated the fate of their buddy, alone and facing a ruthless enemy. The Department of Defense account stipulates that Technical Sergeant John Chapman, an Air Force combat controller, immediately radioed for AC-130 gunship support. It is unclear if that support was for them or Roberts. No matter, as at least one AC-130 converged on Takur Ghar and reported a possible sighting of a handful of enemy combatants carrying or dragging a body.

Razor 04, after inserting its team, arrived at the crash site of Razor 03 some time later. Here they picked up the Night Stalkers and SEALs. One would assume that this combined force would have taken off toward Takur Ghar but instead they headed to Gardez. There has been speculation that the combined weight made the helicopter unsuitable for proper maneuvering. Whatever the reason, orders, injuries or weight restrictions, Razor 04 with five SEAL teammates of Roberts and TSgt Chapman eventually departed to return to the mountaintop. A question does remain; if headquarters knew of Roberts' fall shortly after 0300hrs, why had a quick reaction force (QRF) not been sent immediately? The scenario was reminiscent of one nearly 10 years earlier when a QRF made up of Rangers and Delta endured an 18-hour fire-fight in Somalia after a helicopter had been downed by RPG fire. It took two hours from the time of his fall until Razor 04 arrived near the mountain. Surely other SEALs or Coalition forces such as Danish special operations forces could have been flown in under cover of air support. The answer may have been that logistically it was difficult to provide additional resources as the US military at this point was already stretched to its limits.

Small arms captured in Afghanistan by SEALs.

In any event, Razor 04 decided that landing at the base of the mountain was unacceptable as the difficult ascent would take more hours and steal whatever hope they were holding on to for their buddy's well-being. Time was of the essence. Their only real chance of success was to reinsert in the same proximity of where Razor 03 had taken intense enemy fire. At about 0500 local time, Razor 04 approached the HLZ atop Takur Ghar. Despite enemy fire cutting through the MH-47E, all six members of what had been a "recce" element were safely inserted, and the helicopter, although damaged, returned to base.

With light approaching, the six men moved toward the last known position of their comrade on the high ground. A number of trees dotted the high ground but the two most prominent features were a large rock formation and a tree. As the special operations unit advanced on this area, Chapman and another SEAL from SEAL Team Six engaged two enemy personnel fortified near the tree and killed them. Immediately Chapman was gunned down from a bunker position about 20m away. The Americans engaged the bunker with small arms fire and grenades. During the brief encounter, two SEALs were wounded by shrapnel and gunfire. Having suffered 50 percent casualties, the team withdrew as the al-Qaeda and Taliban fighters engaged them from several locations. Two more of the enemy were killed during the retreat down the northeast of the mountain peak as an AC-130, GRIM 32, provided requested fire support from one of the SEALs. The two wounded commandos took the point during the movement. The SEALs requested immediate assistance. Air Force commando John Chapman's body was left on the mountaintop.

There has been recent documentation that Chapman was not killed upon being shot. Indeed, Sean Naylor argues in his book *Not a Good Day to Die* that none of the SEALs physically checked on the shot AF operator. Instead, as the DEVGRU SEALs retreated down the mountain with their wounded, John Chapman continued the fight. As subsequent Predator footage shows, Chapman entered a bunker and defended it against several al-Qaeda fighters who assaulted the bunker, ultimately killing him. Seemingly when the SEAL leader glanced at Chapman, the dead body on the ground was in fact Neil Roberts – not John Chapman who continued to assault through the objective.

As the situation around Takur Ghar unfolded with Razor 04 inserting SEALs, an Army Ranger QRF was ordered to move to Gardez and be on standby for possible deployment. This was to position them closer to the fight, within 15 minutes' response time. The QRF was assigned to the Night Stalkers' MH-

Naval Special Warfare forces practice close-quarter battle techniques. It has become more common for SEALs to conduct longer-range reconnaissance and combat patrols in land-locked countries such as Afghanistan.

47Es, Razor 01 and Razor 02. Razor 01 carried ten Rangers and three Air Force commandos, one enlisted tactical air controller, a combat controller, and a para-rescueman. Razor 02 carried ten Rangers.

Although today's military forces tend to be micro-managed, surprisingly the QRF had almost no idea as to the situation that caused the chain of events unfolding in front of the very eyes of headquarters personnel. The Department of Defense states that "the QRF had little knowledge about what was actually happening on Takur Ghar due to very limited communications." The most baffling aspect of this fight is simply that the most technologically advanced military in the world was not capable of effectively communicating with its units – although headquarters personnel as far away as the United States could view footage from its unmanned reconnaissance aircraft. The priorities were clearly not in the best interest of the man on the ground fighting for his life. During the flight to Gardez, the hard-pressed SEALs who were withdrawing from the mountaintop requested immediate assistance. The six-man team had one killed and two wounded by this time, a 50 percent casualty rate, and were quickly running out of ammunition. According to official records, headquarters had approved the request and ordered the two helicopters to a nearby location, an "offset" HLZ, but not the same landing zone where Razors 03 and 04 had previously encountered problems. Due to intermittently functioning aircraft communications equipment, the Rangers and helicopter crews never received the "offset" instructions which also hampered attempts to provide tactical situational awareness to the QRF commander aboard Razor 01. Communications problems also plagued headquarters' attempts to determine the true condition of the SEAL team and their exact location. The Rangers continued on plan, believing that the SEALs were still located on top of Takur Ghar, proceeding to the same location where both Razors 03 and 04 had taken enemy fire. At about 0545 local, Razors 01 and 02 flew towards the Takur Ghar landing zone.

Nearly three hours after Navy SEAL Roberts had fallen out of the helicopter, a more suitably sized force, instead of the smaller SEAL team, was about to descend into a prepared squad of al-Qaeda and Taliban fighters who had fortified positions to fight from. And they knew from years of guerrilla warfare that the

This video picture is from Predator Drone footage, taken moments after Chinook Razor 01 carrying the Rangers' quick reaction force to rescue SEAL Roberts was shot down on Takur Ghar. On final approach it was hit on the right side by a rocket-propelled grenade, and by small arms fire from three directions.

The area of operations during Operation *Anaconda*, showing the importance of the mountaintop of Takur Ghar as a vantage point. What started out here as an operation to insert a reconnaissance team turned into a fire-fight in which American special forces clashed with surprisingly well-disciplined guerrillas putting up organized resistance.

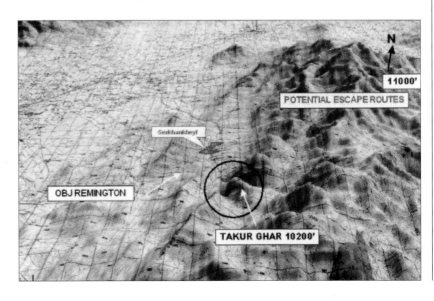

Americans would return for Roberts, dead or alive. It was into these conditions that an unaware quick reaction force was about to enter.

Daylight was approaching as Razor 01 approached the HLZ from the south. On final approach, an RPG round exploded on the right side of the helicopter, while small arms fire peppered it from three directions. By this time, constant surveillance was sending live footage back to headquarters. The footage clearly shows the impact of the grenade round which subsequently forces the pilots into evasive action. Seemingly, the Chinook sustained enough damage to execute a controlled crash landing, dropping the last 10ft, in which the pilots were injured. The right side mini-gunner, Sergeant Phil Svitak, opened fire but was hit by an AK47 round and died almost immediately. The helicopter nose was pointing up the hill toward the main enemy bunkers, where TSgt Chapman had been killed.

Undoubtedly most of the crew were knocked around during the crash but managed to get back on their feet to exit the ramp of the helicopter. Enemy small arms fire raked the fuselage, killing one Ranger inside and another two as they began to emerge from the ramp. One of the Rangers killed a nearby enemy combatant as the Rangers formed a perimeter around the rear of the Chinook. The pilots escaped through the front windows of the crippled helicopter. On footage several fighters can be seen running around the snow-covered area as Rangers are said to have killed another two guerrillas, one with an RPG. Using standard infantry tactics and training, the men attempted to assault the enemy bunker near the top of the hill, but were unable to do so. Too small a force, against probably twice their number, the Rangers must have realized that their position might be overrun. Rather than launching an assault, the Rangers consolidated their position, utilizing nearly every member of the aircraft to help redistribute ammunition and aid in the overall defense. Razor 01's Air Force CCT successfully called for fire on enemy positions to within 50m of their own location. By 0700hrs the QRF was no longer in danger of being overrun as the aerial support proved its worth and the number of al-Qaeda and Taliban fighters was probably no more than a handful by this time.

Sometime shortly after the first QRF helicopter was shot down, Razor 02 was ordered to land in a safer area for further instruction. As the situation grew more desperate around Takur Ghar, with half the QRF dead or wounded and a SEAL team still struggling against a few tenacious fighters, the second chalk of the QRF force was inserted 800m east and 2,000ft below the mountaintop. Requests by the beleaguered SEAL team, located about 1,000m below the top, for the Rangers to come to their aid were rejected as the situation was less immediate than that of the special forces element atop the mountain, who were still in danger of being overrun at this time. Razor 02's single Navy SEAL slogged his way toward his comrades as the Rangers headed toward their objective. Few people realize the extreme difficulties in

NSW forces commonly purchase civilian-manufactured gear as designs are more innovative than standard issue items.

moving across mountain ranges: every step is so much more difficult to take, every breath a struggle. The snow was up to 3ft deep in places and that, combined with the weight of uniform and equipment, made this a daunting task. Unfortunately for some of the Rangers, many of them wore "snivel" gear against the cold and now were paying the price for it, overheating during the arduous climb to the top. As time went by and the men became more exhausted, they decided to throw out their back Kevlar plate, part of the Ranger body armor. But first they had to receive permission from headquarters! Official sources say the Rangers were also under heavy mortar barrage. The climb lasted two to three hours and it was 1030hrs before they consolidated into their position around the helicopter. The brutish climb took its toll, but the special forces team drew up hasty plans to assault and eliminate the threat barely 50m in front of them.

Camouflage netting disguises a SEAL hidesite in mountain terrain in Afghanistan, 2002.

The harsh terrain and climate of Afghanistan are not areas commonly associated with Navy SEALs. It was up terrain similar to this that a single Navy SEAL slogged his way toward his comrades during the fight on Takur Ghar amid snow that was up to 3ft deep in places.

The Air Force CCT called in a last airstrike on the enemy bunkers and, with two machine guns providing suppression fire, seven Rangers stormed the hill as quickly as they could in the knee-deep snow, shooting and throwing grenades. The attack lasted only a few minutes and killed several enemy personnel. The bodies of Roberts and Chapman were discovered in a pillbox or bunker-type fortification. Having secured the immediate area, the Americans moved their position to the very top of the mountain and reconsolidated their perimeter. Unfortunately, their position was exposed to fire from another ridgeline a few hundred meters away, wounding two more soldiers. More airstrikes were called in, finally either killing the enemy or forcing them to retreat.

The wreckage of Chinook Razor 01 on Takur Ghar. When the aircraft was hit the pilots carried out a controlled crash landing, during which the Chinook dropped the last 10ft on to the mountaintop. The right side mini-gunner opened fire but was hit by an AK47 round and died almost immediately.

Senior Airman Jason Cunningham, the Air Force pararescueman, eventually died of his wounds after repeated calls for emergency medevacs were denied by headquarters. The explanation for this decision was that they did not want to risk other helicopters getting shot down during daylight hours, that the enemy air defense and ground situation in the vicinity of Takur Ghar did not lend itself to another daylight rescue attempt using helicopters. The isolated special forces team had to wait for nightfall. Sporadic mortar and small arms fire kept them busy.

Great credit has been given to other American and Coalition special forces teams that poured in fire mission requests throughout the day to help their comrades on Takur Ghar. Hundreds upon hundreds of al-Qaeda and Taliban fighters were claimed to have been killed. Subsequent interviews revealed that these numbers were probably not accurate at all, but that instead maybe a few dozen were killed.

Nearly 18 hours after Navy SEAL Roberts fell out at Takur Ghar and triggered the desperate rescue attempts, the men airlifted off the mountain with everyone on board, dead and alive.

Operation *Anaconda* continued for another 19 days.

Members of Special Boat Team Twenty-Two (SBT 22) show their capabilities at Stennis, Mississippi, on October 23, 2003, as they practice narrow river beach extractions under hostile fire conditions. SBT 22's main task is to conduct special operations in riverine environments. Special Warfare Combatant-craft Crewmen (SWCC) operate and maintain the state-of-the-art, high-performance boats and ships used to support Navy SEALs and special operations missions. (US Navy photo)

Takur Ghar timeline

March 2   US commanders plan to insert commandos atop 10,200ft Takur Ghar. The towering peak offers a clear view of activities in the valleys below.

March 3   Two MH-47E Chinook helicopters take off late at night from Gardez, dozens of miles away. Their mission is to insert SEAL teams for observation posts.

March 4

0300hrs   One Chinook approaches its helicopter landing zone atop Takur Ghar and is hit by RPG and small arms fire. Evasive action causes Navy SEAL Neil Roberts to fall out.

0300–0500hrs Roberts is killed by al-Qaeda and Taliban fighters.

0500hrs   The other members of Roberts' team, who have boarded another Chinook, advance on Takur Ghar and are driven off. Air Force Technical Sergeant John Chapman is killed and his body left behind.

0545hrs   Another Chinook carrying a quick reaction force (QRF) is shot down on the mountain. A number are wounded and four killed.

0700hrs   The Rangers consolidate their positions and are no longer in danger of being overrun. The second half of the QRF climb up the mountain.

1030hrs   The combined QRF attacks enemy positions and recovers the bodies of Chapman and Roberts.

2015hrs   Night-time evacuation. Another special forces member bleeds to death as headquarters refuses daylight evacuation. Arrive at Gardez one hour later.

US Navy SEAL Neil Roberts, 32, of Woodland, California, during his naval service. He died surrounded by al-Qaeda and Taliban fighters after being stranded alone on top of Takur Ghar, Afghanistan, on March 4, 2002. The subsequent fight on the mountain claimed the lives of six other US servicemen.

NAVY SEALS KILLED IN ACTION 1983–2003

Grenada, 1983

Four SEALs were killed during Operation *Urgent Fury*, the invasion of Grenada. Unable to carry out what should have been a standard naval commando infiltration, the insertion of frogmen via submarine, the SEALs had to make a night-time parachute jump, their task made all the more hazardous by deteriorating weather, the unpredictability of the sea, and their heavy gear. Those who died were Machinist Mate First Class Kenneth J. Butcher; Quartermaster First Class Kevin E. Lundberg; Senior Chief Engineman Robert R. Schamberger; and Hull Technician First Class Stephen L. Morris.

Panama, 1989

During Operation *Just Cause*, the invasion of Panama intended to oust its leader Manuel Noriega, Navy SEALs were caught in a fire-fight at Patilla

A family photograph of Navy SEAL Chief Hospital Corpsman Matthew J. Bourgeois, 35, from Tallahassee, Florida. Chief Bourgeois was stationed in Norfolk, Virginia, and deployed to Afghanistan in support of Operation *Enduring Freedom*. He was killed on Wednesday, March 27, 2002.

FAR RIGHT **Navy Photographer's Mate 1st Class Petty Officer David M. Tapper, 32, from Camden County, New Jersey, was fatally wounded in Afghanistan on August 20, 2003.**

airport. Those who died were Lieutenant John Connors, Chief Petty Officer (ENC) Donald McFaul; Torpedoman's Mate 2nd Class Issac Rodriguez; and Boatswain's Mate 1st Class Chris Tilghman.

Afghanistan

Among those killed were Interior Communications Electrician 1st Class Thomas E. Retzer, 30, wounded after his convoy made contact with enemy forces outside Gardez during Operation *Enduring Freedom*. He was transported to Bagram Air Base hospital, where he died of his wounds. Retzer, who was part of a Virginia Beach-based SEAL team, was a 10-year veteran.

Navy Photographer's Mate 1st Class Petty Officer David M. Tapper, 32, a member of a Virginia Beach-based SEAL team, was fatally wounded in 2003 after his convoy made contact with enemy forces near Orgun, in Paktika Province. He was taken to Bagram Air Base hospital where he died. Tapper was a 13-year veteran.

Chief Hospital Corpsman Matthew J. Bourgeois, 35, was killed in 2002 while conducting small unit training at a remote location near Qandahar. Stationed in Norfolk, Virginia, Chief Bourgeois was killed after apparently stepping on an enemy land mine.

OPERATION *IRAQI FREEDOM*

The largest number of SEALs and Special Warfare Combatant Craft Crewmen (SWCC) in history was deployed during the invasion of Iraq. NSW forces conducted numerous special reconnaissance and direct action missions. They secured the southern oil infrastructures of the Al Faw peninsula and the offshore gas and oil terminals; cleared the Khawr Abd Allah and Khawr Az Zubayr waterways and enabled unmolested access to the vital port city of Umm Qasr. Other missions included reconnaissance of the Shat Al Arab waterway; the capture of high-value targets, raids on suspected chemical, biological and radiological sites; and the first POW rescue since World War Two.

The *San Diego Union-Tribune*'s Jim Crawley wrote a more detailed article on the missions conducted by NSW forces during Operation Iraqi Freedom, on June 27, 2003:

"Dodging a web of high-voltage power lines, Air Force special operations helicopters hovered over the hydroelectric dam, 57 miles northeast of Baghdad, as crewmen kicked thick ropes out the doors.

"Under a moonless April night, dark figures quickly rappelled to the ground. Several dozen Navy SEALs and Polish Grom commandos split into small groups and sprinted to predetermined locations on Mukarayin Dam, an adjacent power station and several buildings. Within minutes, they located and held the dam's watchmen and power-plant operators, but it would take hours to search the massive structure for explosives and potential saboteurs. 'They were sort of startled by the commandos' sudden apearance', recalled Commander Tom Schibler, a San Diego-based SEAL who was operations officer for the Navy commandos in Iraq. However, the Iraqis didn't resist and no enemy troops or bombs were found, so the commandos let the dam operators continue their work. For five days, the commandos guarded the isolated dam site to prevent Fedayeen Saddam irregulars or Ba'athist loyalists from damaging or destroying the dam and possibly flooding Baghdad downstream. For the first time, Schibler and others this week described several missions that local SEALs and special-warfare boat crews conducted during Operation *Iraqi Freedom*. They cracked open the door on their world of covert operations, disclosing in general terms the dam occupation in April, the capture of offshore oil terminals and the clearing of Iraq's only deep-water estuary in March. They also touched on other wartime missions – sniper v. sniper duels with Fedayeen Saddam loyalists in Baghdad, saving Army Pfc. Jessica Lynch, behind-the-lines reconnaissance and searching for weapons of mass destruction – but declined to give details, saying those missions are still classified.

SEAL Team Three and 41 Commando on a joint training exercise in Kuwait.

"The Iraq war, coming on the heels of the special operations-dominated Operation *Enduring Freedom* in Afghanistan, showed how the Navy's special-warfare units could become key players in a full-scale war, said Commander Kerry Metz, who planned many of the SEALs' Iraq missions. In Operation *Desert Storm*, the first war with Iraq, the SEALs were peripheral to the main action, said Schibler, who served in that conflict. This time, 'we were very central' to the war effort, he said. Nearly 250 SEALs were deployed in and around Iraq – the largest single deployment since Vietnam. In all, about 500 naval special-warfare personnel, including special crewmen who operated high-speed boats that transport commandos, intelligence and communications specialists and even a public affairs officer, were sent to Kuwait and Iraq. 'The missions were such that they required more forces than we customarily were used to operating with, and having more forces gave us...the ability to sustain operations and conduct multiple operations simultaneously,' Schibler said.

"In the past, special operations forces have supported conventional troops, undertaking unusual or dangerous missions with little or no assistance from regular troops. However, in Iraq, conventional forces assisted the SEALs, Schibler said. 'We had incredible support from the regular, big Navy, from ships, helicopters, planes, other support aircraft, even a (British) Royal Marine commando group, surveillance platforms,' he said."

The *San Diego Union-Tribune*'s Jim Crawley continued: "The capture of a northern Iraq dam brought together a mixed group of forces, including US Air Force aircraft and Polish commandos, under the SEALs' command. Military commanders worried that Mukarayin Dam could be sabotaged. 'There was no burning activity at the dam, but you have this big, fat target,' Schibler said. 'It was just sitting there until someone decides to blow it up or opens up the floodgates, flooding Baghdad.' After planning and rehearsing the takeover for several days, the commandos crammed inside several Pave Low special operations helicopters for a nearly five-hour flight from their Kuwait base to the dam. On the way, each helicopter had to be refueled in midair by a KC 130 tanker. It was during the rappel that the commandos' only casualty of the war occurred. A Polish soldier fell, breaking his leg.

"While the dam seizure was one of the final acts during the major combat phase of the war, the SEALs and their Polish allies also participated in one of the first actions of the war. In simultaneous attacks on the war's first night, using helicopters and high-speed boats crewed by sailors from Coronado's Naval Amphibious Base, SEALs and Groms captured Iraq's two offshore oil terminals in the northern Persian Gulf, two valve stations, and a pipeline and pumping facility onshore. The operation prevented the Iraqis from blowing up the critical oil structures, which would have polluted the Persian Gulf and slowed reconstruction.

"After the oil terminals were taken, the SEALs and boat crews switched jobs, clearing a path for warships and cargo vessels into Iraq. Lieutenant Jake Heller said that for eight days, he led a small flotilla of high-speed Mark V craft and 35ft long, rigid hulled inflatable boats in the narrow Khawr Az Zubayr waterway that connects Umm Qasr, Iraq's only deep-water port, to the Persian Gulf. 'Our mission was the clearance of the waterway,' Heller said. It wasn't an easy task. The SEALs captured several vessels loaded with mines, including hard-to-detect Italian Mantra mines that could have sunk US or British warships. The estuary was a graveyard of derelict hulls – about 100 vessels, many rusted and partially submerged. Each vessel, whether a manned fishing dhow or a rusted hull, had to be searched, Heller said.

"Tides rose and fell a dozen feet, exposing dangerous shoals. Tall reeds concealed the shoreline.

Then, while a giant dust storm blanketed Iraq, forcing the ground war to a standstill, gale-force winds of 55 knots buffeted the SEALs' small, open craft. 'Those guys were getting battered,' Heller said. 'We were in enemy territory with death squads taking shots at us and with limited or no visibility. A little bad luck either way and things could have been ugly.' The special-boat crewmen, who were recognized only 18 months ago as a separate Navy specialty, showed their worth in Iraq, Heller said. 'The special-boat-team community is young, and we're still growing and developing and becoming more professional. I think we took some leaps and bounds.'

"The larger SEAL community also got a boost from the war, the officers said, because more special operators are now combat veterans. 'It provided our guys with experience in this sort of very, very fuzzy situation,' Schibler said. The conflict 'showed a lot of our younger operators that (warfare) is not all black-and-white. The bad guys aren't all black-and-white. The missions aren't all black-and-white.'"

Under enemy fire conditions, Special Boat Team Twenty Two (SBT 22) personnel undergo training on narrow river beach extraction at Stennis, Mississippi, on October 23, 2003. Special Warfare Combatant-craft Crewmen (SWCC) focus on clandestine infiltration and extraction of SEALs and other special operations forces, providing dedicated, rapid mobility in shallow water areas as well as open water environments. (US Navy photo)

SEAL TERMINOLOGY

5320 A basic Combat Swimmer or BUD/S graduate

5326 Designation for a Trident wearer

ASDS Advanced SEAL Delivery System. A "dry" mini-submersible that transports a SEAL squad from a host platform, either surface ship or submarine, to an objective area

Bottom sample Collecting soil sample of bottom surface to test suitability for amphibious vehicles. Usually conducted within 21ft of beach as boats or vehicles will not get stuck that far out

Brown shirt A BUD/S student who is post Hell Week, sometimes called a brown skirt

Bull frog Most senior frog, in terms of time in service, not rank

CQB/CQC Close-quarters combat

CQD Close-quarters defense

CRRC Combat Rubber Raiding Craft, also known as Z-Bird, Duck, Rubber Duck, Zodie, F-470 Zodiac

Dive Mask Not goggles

DPV Desert Patrol Vehicle, Rat Patrol

Dräger LAR, German underwater rebreather, closed circuit scuba

Drop down Assume the push-up position but also used jokingly between teammates when someone makes a mistake

Dry Deck Shelter The DDS hangar module will be flooded, pressurized to the surrounding sea pressure, and a large door is opened to allow for launch and recovery of the vehicle

E&R Escape and evade, evade and recover

Fathom Six feet is one fathom

Fins Not flippers

Get wet and sandy A Sugar Cookie (see below)

GOPLATS Gas/oil platforms

Grinder Parade field, slang for center of BUD/S compound

Helo Not chopper

H-Gear Standard H harness-type web gear

Hook and climb Boarding a moving ship by climbing up a narrow aluminum ladder

HOOYAH Navy SEAL war cry equivalent to the Rangers' Hooah or Marines' Oorah

Hydro(graphic) Recon Coastal reconnaissance, usually conducted from the $3\frac{1}{2}$ fathom curve up to the high water mark. Underwater hydro work would be normally conducted with scuba gear. There are two different types of hydros – combat or admin (non-combat). Hydro Recon can be conducted perpendicular or parallel to the area

IBS Inflatable boat small, old-school UDT rubber boat, used today but only by BUD/S students

Jacob's Ladder Rope ladder, tossed off the ramp end of a helo

Jock Up/Jocked Up Get gear on, get suited up

K-Duck Kangaroo, refers to an inflated zodiac or other boat being attached by a D-ring to the bottom of a helicopter for transportation

Knock'em Out Do push-ups until the instructor gets tired

Lead Line Used to measure water's surface

Limp Duck Boat is carried inside a helo and inflated in water

Limpet Underwater mine attached to the underside of a ship. Can be effectively carried by a combat swimmer. Two limpets per swimmer. Can be attached to harbor areas/piers

NAVSPECWAR Naval Special Warfare

Niland "The land of Nye", west coast desert training facility

OBM Outboard motor

OTB Over-the-beach

OTH Over-the-horizon

Phase Up/Class Up First day of First Phase, official class start

PLO Patrol leader's order

RHIB Rigid Hull Inflatable Boat

Ring Out To "ring the bell" at BUD/S when an attendee wants to quit or drop on request

San Clemente Island "The Rock", Camp Huey, where no one hears your screams

SEALs prepare to embark on a mission supported by Marine Corps helicopters.

SBU Special Boat Unit/s. Also known as Boat Drivers or SBShoe. Shoe or Black Shoe is a slang term for a regular Navy fleet person. A non-SEAL can be a Diver or an Airdale which refers to the Naval Aviation community, sometimes referred to as Brown Shoes

SDV SEAL Delivery Vehicle

SEAL Trident Wearer, Team Guy, Frog, Frogman

Silver Strand or just **The Strand** Highway between Imperial Beach and Coronado proper

SPECWAR Special Warfare

SPIE Rig Special purpose insertion/extraction

Sugar Cookie Art of rolling in the sand, must be wet, useful for camouflage of individual and gear

Trident Budweiser, Bird

Trident Board An oral interview which has no set length of time, to challenge basic knowledge before being awarded the Trident

Twin 80s How the US Navy dives open circuit scuba when wearing tanks with compressed air

VBSS Visit Board Search Seizure

VSW Very shallow water

VSWMCM Very shallow water mine counter measures

White Shirt Pre-training/pre-trainee, indoctrination and First Phase BUD/S until completion of Hell Week

BIBLIOGRAPHY

Adkin, Mark, *Urgent Fury: The Battle for Grenada*, Lexington Books, 1989
Bahmanyar, Mir, *US Army Ranger 1983–2002* (Warrior 65), Osprey Publishing, Oxford, 2003.
Baker, Caleb, *et al*, editors, *Commando Operations*, Time Life Books, New York, 1991
Dockery, Kevin, *SEALs in Action*, Avon Books, New York, 1991
Flanagan, Lt. Gen. Edward M. Jr., *Battle for Panama: Inside Operation Just Cause*, Brassey's, New York, 1993
Halberstadt, Hans, *US Navy SEALs in Action*, MBI, Osceola, 1995
Halberstadt, Hans, *US Navy SEALs*, MBI, Osceola, 1993
Kelly, Orr, *Never Fight Fair!*, Presidio Press, Novato, 1995
Marcinko, Richard, with John Weisman, *Rogue Warrior*, Pocket Books, New York, 1992

McConnell, Malcolm, *Just Cause*, St Martin's Press, New York, 1991

Nadel, Joel, with Wright, *J.R., Special Men and Special Mission: Inside American Special Operations Forces 1945 to the Present*, Greenhill Books, London, 1994

Naylor, Sean, *Not a Good Day to Die: The Untold Story of Operation Anaconda*, Berkley Books, New York, 2005

Padden, Ian, *US Navy Seals*, Bantam Books, New York, 1985

Rottman, Gordon, *Panama 1989–90* (Elite 37), Osprey Publishing, London, 1991

Russell, Lee E., and Mendez, M. Albert, *Grenada 1983* (Men-at-Arms 159), Osprey Publishing, London, 1985

Stubblefield, Gary, *Inside the US Navy SEALs*, MBI, Osceola, 1995

Websites

www.suasponte.com
www.navyseals.com
www.specialoperations.com
www.defenselink.mil

THE PLATES

A: US NAVY SEALs 1983–2004

A1: BUD/S student
The first step in becoming a Navy SEAL is the arduous Basic Underwater Demolition course in California. This student wears his basic BDU, in his principal training environment – water.

A2: US Navy SEAL
This US Navy SEAL wears standard woodland pattern DBDUs with a modular load bearing vest. He is armed with an M-4 carbine.

A3: Special Warfare Combatant Craft Crewman
Although these men are not SEALs, they actively support SEAL missions throughout the world.

A4: Naval Special Warfare Command badge

A5: The Navy SEAL Trident
The Navy SEAL Trident is also known as the "Budweiser" as the insignia looks similar to the logo of the American beer manufacturer. This insignia is awarded to fully-fledged members of SEAL teams.

A6: SEAL Team 1 **A7:** ST 2 **A8:** ST 3 **A9:** ST 4 **A10:** ST 5 **A11:** ST 6 (DevGru) **A12:** ST 7 **A13:** ST 8 **A14:** ST 10.

B: GRENADA OCTOBER 1983, OPERATION *URGENT FURY*

B1: Navy SEAL, winter battledress
The Navy SEAL on the left wears the relatively new winter battledress uniform (BDU) in the woodland pattern. The summer BDUs are made much lighter. The trouser legs are loose and rolled up. He carries a canvas H-harness configuration with additional ammunition pouches. Canvas tends to disintegrate in wet climates.

B2: Navy SEAL
Over his BDU, this SEAL wears the traditional nylon webgear based on the Alice system. The Vietnam-era Jungle boot was standard issue for military forces and featured a mud-resistant sole as well as a metal sole insert to combat bamboo spikes commonly associated with booby traps during the war in Vietnam. He carries the M16 standard infantry rifle for the US military with a 20-round magazine.

B3: BTR 60 APC
This armored personnel carrier was the first in the line of Russian eight-wheeled APCs and was first developed in the late 1950s. Although continually improved upon by a succession of different APCs, it continued to exist until the Warsaw Pact. The BTR 60 was the standard mechanized vehicle for ground troops.

B4: Fast-roping
SEALs fast-roping out of a Black Hawk helicopter. At the time the Black Hawk was considered top secret and replaced the ageing Huey although only special operations units used them in the early 1980s. Fast-roping also replaced the more traditional insertion method of rappelling, perfected by special forces units during the Vietnam War. Fast-roping has undergone a few changes. At times it was discouraged to use the feet and the individual would simply grab on to the nylon rope, push out and lock his arms, allowing weight and gravity to do the rest. However, fast-roping with heavier gear such as body armor and machine guns was far more difficult. Whatever the technique, mass fast-roping, four or five men on a single rope, is usually difficult and safety measures have been introduced in an effort to reduce injuries in training.

C: ZODIAC OPERATIONS CHINOOK

In case of emergency a quick getaway may lead to seemingly odd situations, but USSOCOM personnel regularly train under difficult conditions to ensure they are able to execute these very same maneuvers during combat operations. Here a small team of Navy SEALs races into the back of an awaiting Chinook helicopter with its ramp lowered. The MH-47E Special Operations Aircraft (SOA) is a derivative of the Boeing CH-47 Chinook and is seeing an increased amount of use in Afghanistan due to its ability to climb to higher altitudes than the smaller Black Hawk helicopters. Some of the modifications include increased fuel capacity and radar operating systems. This craft has been specifically modified to allow special operations infiltration and exfiltration in adverse weather conditions. The three types of CH-47 in the Army inventory are the CH-47D, the MH-47D, and the MH-47E. The MH-47D and the MH-47E are air refuelable, which allows long-range penetration, medium-assault helicopter support for special operations forces. Depending on the version, a CH-47 can travel 1,100–2,000nm without needing to be refueled. During Operation *Just Cause*, CH-47s conducted H-hour assaults to support other elements who were air-landing special operations forces to disrupt enemy responses and seize key facilities. During Operation *Desert Storm*, the CH-47 conducted infiltration and exfiltration of special forces and combat search and rescue of downed pilots.

D: OPERATION *JUST CAUSE*, PATILLA AIRPORT, 1989

D1: Navy SEAL with customized gear

This figure wears traditional battledress uniform and Alice webgear, with numerous added ammunition pouches and two-quart canteens. This Navy SEAL sports a special operations favorite – the CAR 15, which has a collapsible stock and fires the same round, 5.56mm, as the M16. He carries a bandoleer filled with additional ammo and has a LAW primarily used against light armored vehicles, bunkers and enemy troops.

D2: Commando with M60E

This naval commando carries the shortened M60E and thus represents the firepower of his team. A shortened barrel reduces the weight, although the weapon may not be able to engage targets at as great a distance as the unaltered version. He too wears the standard issue webgear, customized for his weapons' needs, and carries several grenades. One of the main reasons a machine gunner would carry the heavy grenades is that in the event that enemy personnel have not yet discovered the gunner, he can throw a grenade and maim or distract the enemy without giving away his position.

OPPOSITE **Temporary bathing facilities in Afghanistan. Although often romanticized, living conditions can be spartan at best when forces are on deployment.**

RIGHT **SEAL team member participates in an exercise during Forward Air Controller (FAC) School, Fallon, Nevada, on June 2, 2003. SEALS used their skills identifying potential targets for special operations forces and warning coalition ground forces of nearby enemy activity during Operation *Iraqi Freedom*.**

D3: Learjet

The private jet was eventually disabled by intent or accident during the firefight at Patilla airport. A LAW rocket may have caused the damage to the airplane's fuselage. Small arms fire has peppered the craft as well. The Navy SEALs poured massive quantities of bullets into the hangar. Some after-action reports criticized the lack of fire discipline. Traditionally, suppressive fire does not mean putting large amounts of ammunition toward the enemy positions, but rather to take well-aimed shots, to the best abilities and circumstances. As all special forces units have to carry their ammunition to their areas of operation, fire discipline is absolutely crucial. Six years earlier when the SEALs successfully repulsed enemy forces at the Governor General's house on Grenada, their ammunition ran dangerously low.

D4: Civilian Guard

This man represents the private army purchased by Manuel Noriega for his personal protection as well as protection of his property. In this case, the private guard is armed with an American manufactured M16.

E: OPERATION *ENDURING FREEDOM*, AFGHANISTAN, 2002

E1: Desert Patrol Vehicle

The DPV is an excellent means of high-speed transportation/patrolling. The vehicle can be equipped with a variety of weapons, making it an excellent weapons platform. Nonetheless, dangers are profound when traveling at night and at high speeds. During Operation *Desert Storm* at least one special operations forces member was seriously injured when his vehicle landed awkwardly. Navy SEALs attend different driving schools to enhance their ability to handle a variety of vehicles.

E2: Civilian vehicle

There are times when special forces units use civilian vehicles in their combat operations. There have been reports of vehicles being marked with United Nations logos.

E3: Soldier, German special operations forces

German special operations forces participated in several combat patrols with Navy SEALs. The recent Global War on Terrorism has seen an enormous increase in allied special operations cooperation. German units have acquired an excellent reputation within the special operations community. Although they have taken part in hostage rescue missions, this is the first time German forces have participated in combat operations since World War II.

E4: Navy SEAL disguised as an Afghan fighter

Although to the untrained eye at a distance these disguises may work, the tell-tale sign of high-speed gear and weaponry make it clear that this is a special operations

The variety of SEAL gear and uniforms shown here demonstrates the great latitude given to NSW forces over their personal equipment. The fast and furious nature of most special operations missions has led to the practice of attaching pouches to body armor to double as webgear. This can make it difficult for the SEAL to "hug" the ground amid enemy fire.

forces member. Besides, the local population would probably have an excellent intelligence system in place.

E5: Navy SEAL, desert camouflage

This SEAL is dressed in the now familiar three-pattern desert camouflage uniform with a broad-rimmed boonie hat. Note his headset beneath the headgear.

E6: Member of Danish special operations forces

Danish special operations forces have enjoyed a particularly close relationship with their American counterparts. They acted as a stand-by quick reaction force during the Battle of Takur Ghar but were not deployed.

F: TAKUR GHAR, OPERATION *ANACONDA*, MARCH 2002

Hypothetical recreation of the desperate attempt by a small SEAL team to gain a foothold atop Takur Ghar in Afghanistan. SEAL commando Neil Roberts has by this time been killed and dragged off to a nearby bunker. Approximately 12 al-Qaeda and Taliban fighters were spread around the small saddle top of the mountain in anticipation that the Americans would send relief forces. One of these fighters is seen in the foreground (**F1**). The difficult terrain and small numbers of SEAL operators made their task nearly impossible but the dedication of the men to their missing comrade is commendable and should be expected of all men in war. Seemingly no other force was available to augment the SEALs. If reinforcing them was unsuitable then any diversionary "false" insertion might have been helpful, although time was of the essence and any complex plan would have taken up precious time. At this point, Navy SEAL Roberts had been lost for over two hours. Many of the SEALs are wearing white camoflague, but others, including Technical Sergeant John Chapman, the Air Force combat controller (**F2**), are dressed in desert cammies. Chapman is carrying a rucksack with his communications gear necessary for co-ordinating air support. He is firing an M4.

G: OPERATION *IRAQI FREEDOM*, IRAQ, 2002

Great latitude is given to Navy SEALs' personal attire and gear. More often than not they purchase high-quality and specialty manufactured equipment to complement their standard issues. Shown here are the variety of clothing worn by SEALs throughout the campaigns in Afghanistan and Iraq. Civilian and military contractors will at times donate their equipment for "unofficial" testing. At other times, greater discounts are offered. Over the past few years, personal body armor has made it difficult to carry large rucksacks. The need for protection, coupled with the fast and furious nature of most special operations missions, has led to an increase in the practice of attaching pouches to the body armor to double as webgear. The Molle and Rack systems have long been touted for their flexibility in customizing personal gear; however, the increase of chest pouches has made it difficult for the soldier to "hug" the ground, thus exposing him to more enemy fire. Body armor is essential to modern day shock troops and eventually gear will evolve to make it more comfortable and smart without risking the carrier's life.

H: OPERATION *IRAQI FREEDOM*, IRAQ, 2002: GOPLATS

Gas/oil platform seizure is routinely practiced. The favorite method tends to be fast-rope insertions although the mission can also be executed via helicopter, scuba, or through other amphibious means. In simultaneous attacks on the war's first night, using helicopters and high-speed boats crewed by sailors from Coronado's Naval Amphibious Base, SEALs and Polish commandos, the Groms, captured Iraq's two offshore oil terminals in the northern Persian Gulf, two valve stations, and a pipeline and pumping facility onshore. The operation prevented the Iraqis from blowing up the critical oil structures, which would have polluted the Persian Gulf. One of the most difficult tasks for Navy SEALs is a waterborne seizure of a GOPLAT. The extreme weather conditions usually associated with water, the exhaustion of the approach, and the actual assault climb can be excruciating. This is a true Navy SEAL mission although with the advent of heliborne assaults one wonders for how much longer this will remain a pure Naval Special Warfare mission, as it becomes more common for SEALs to conduct longer-range reconnaissance and combat patrols in land-locked countries such as Afghanistan.

ABOVE **A soldier of the 1st Battalion, 87th Infantry mans a tower at the compound of the Provincial Reconstruction Team in Gardez, Afghanistan. Chairman of the Joint Chiefs of Staff, Air Force General Richard B. Myers, visited the facility.**

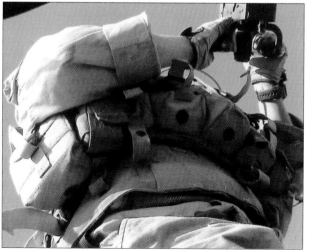

LEFT **Another example of a chest pouch configuration. Note the large draining holes on the bottom part of each pouch.**

INDEX